Cultural China Series

Wang Guangxi

CHINESE KUNGFU

Masters, Schools and Combats

Translated by Han Huizhi, Wang Wenliang & Kang Jian

CHINA
INTERCONTINENTAL
PRESS

图书在版编目（CIP）数据

中国功夫／王广西著，王萌整理；韩慧枝等译.—北京：五洲传播出版社，2010.1

ISBN 978-7-5085-1317-1

I.中... II.①王...②韩... III.武术－概况－中国－英文 IV.G852

中国版本图书馆CIP数据核字（2008）第058040号

CHINESE KUNGFU
Masters, Schools and Combats

Author: Wang Guangxi

Compiler: Wang Meng

Translator: Han Huizhi, Wang Wenliang & Kang Jian

Executive Editor: Gao Lei

Art Director: Tian Lin

Publisher: China Intercontinental Press (6 Beixiaomachang, Lianhuachi Donglu, Haidian District, Beijing 100038, China)

Tel: 86-10-58891281

Website: www.cicc.org.cn

Printer: C&C Joint Printing Co., (Beijing) Ltd.

Format: 720×965mm 1/16

Edition: Jan. 2010, 1st edition, 1st print run

Price: RMB 90.00 (*yuan*)

Contents

Foreword

Wushu, the Chinese martial art form known as kungfu in the West, is a valuable cultural heritage of Chinese people and contribution to human civilization. Wushu, often used in the form of combat, consists of several different kinds of movements. The Chinese people's determination to win and strong character traits are reflected in the fierce body combat (which appear in the form of postulated and imitation combat).

Wushu reflects the character of Chinese people and applies their unique understanding of theory and principle to combat. It differs from European and American boxing, which are widely known to be violent; and from Japanese Karate, which possesses the cultural characteristics of an island country; it is also different from Muay Thai, which has characteristics of strong jungle fury. Wushu is a particular balance between hard and soft, and extrinsic and intrinsic values, which not only show the robust beauty of one's figure, but also

Stretch out view of cooper pot with conviviality, archery and water-and-land warfare pattern (Warring States Period, Chengdu, Sichuan province)

the meaning of profound elegance. Apart from simply combat techniques, martial arts are rooted in Chinese philosophy, containing ancient Chinese philosophers' understanding of life and the universe.

Wushu, which aims to improve health and self-defense, begins by fostering one's moral character. The martial art movements are physically demonstrated while internal thoughts are static and neutralized; the energy is thus fierce on the outside and quiet on the inside, static on the inside and dynamic on the outside. Wushu is not fond of bravery, nor fighting. Like still waters, peace and quiet is considered the highest realm of martial arts.

Having survived the vicissitudes of life while maintaining all of its strength and vitality, some even believe Wushu to be the epitome of Chinese traditional culture and national spirit.

The Origins of Martial Arts

Wushu was historically termed "quan yong" or martial arts. But fairly recently, the Chinese government changed the term to "guoshu" during the Republican Period (1912–1949) while foreigners call it "kungfu." The Chinese martial art was rooted in the war between humans and animals among the tribes. An excerpt from *The Book of Poetry* traces the martial art back to the Spring and Autumn Period (770 BC–476 BC). Further passages from *Zhuangzi* recorded over three thousand swordsmen of King Zhao (in the late Qin Dynasty) fought with each other day and night, and never grew tired of fighting. During the Han Dynasty (202 BC–AD 220), the practice of martial arts made remarkable progress. Many a paintings on relief stone sculptures from the Han Dynasty, which were unearthed in Henan, describe the martial arts movements in varied forms, including similarities to fencing, painting, sword playing,

Mirror with human-animal fighting patterns, the Qin Dynasty (221–206), Yunmeng, Hunan province

Hongmen Banquet—Xiang Zhuang performing sword dance

The drawing portrays the famous story of Hongmen Banquet in Chinese history. In 206 BC, two states—Chu and Han—contended for hegemony after the Qin Dynasty ended. Liubang, King of Han state, went to Hongmen to meet Xiang Yu, King of Chu state. During the banquet, Xiang Zhuang performed the sword dance as a cover for his attempt on Liu Bang's life.

Martial arts and hunting drawings, hollow brick relief, the Eastern Han Dynasty (25–220), Zhengzhou, Henan province

Qigong Jade Inscription

Qigong Jade Inscription
This is a small jade column with 12 sides of the early Warring States period that is now kept in the Tianjin History Museum. There are 45 characters engraved on the jade, recording the methods and directions of Qigong practice, similar to the subsequent Zhoutiangong, and it is the earliest and moest complete Qigong method ever found in China. The internal strength in wushu is related with it.
This inscription means: when exercising Qi energy, one must take a deep breath and store more energy to enable one's Qi to extend to the lower part of one's body. When qi moves to a certain position (pubic region), one must stop to make Qi sink. Then breathe out the Qi in reverse direction, like grass in the bud growing upward. With mutual movement and exchange, if one exercises Qi along this direction, one can live long; if against this direction, one will die.

snatching spears empty-handed, and bayonet practice using a sword and lance—all of which reflect the "solo" and "sparring" forms of martial arts.

Following the Spring and Autumn Period, Taoism was formed, and famous Chinese philosopher Laozi advocated for the "renewal of oneself while embracing perfect peace," and for the "unity of body and mind while concentrating on breathing" while Zhuangzi essentially proposed the idea of "exhaling the old and inhaling the new." The Xingqi Yupei Ming, or the *Qi* Circulation Inscription, from the Warring States Period (475–221 BC) recorded the *qi*-promoting method. Laozi and Zhuangzi's theory of "cultivating *qi*" combined the theory of yin-and-yang with the five elements: metal, wood, water, fire and earth. This became the training basis for the internal exercise of Wushu. Some of Laozi's philosophical theories, such as restricting action through silence, conquering the unyielding with the yielding and "cats hide their paws" were absorbed by various styles of Wushu and were considered the

Bare hands tussling with lance, stone relief, the Han Dynasty, Nanyang, Henan province

principles of internal styles of martial arts.

Cultivating extrinsic and intrinsic values and unifying the body and soul make up the basic characteristics of Wushu. Throughout the process of historical development, martial arts have integrated the promotion of *qi* while martial artists have worked to transfer the potential energy in their bodies though systematic *qi*-promoting training to achieve the goal of "mind leads *qi* and *qi* promotes the strength." During the Song (960–1279) and Yuan (1271–1368) Dynasties, martial arts began to incorporating the *qi*-promoting methods. The Shaolin kungfu matured by the end of Ming Dynasty (1368–1644) and the Wudang styles grew out of the same period; both are seen as natural trends in the historical development of martial arts.

Principles of Wushu

Tiger-shaped stone, from China's Scenery by Okada Gyokuzan, published in 1802

Li Guang, a famous general of the Western Han Dynasty (BC 206–AD 25), shoots an arrow deeply into a stone in the shape of a crouching tiger on a night patrol.

The principles of martial arts are also the disciplines of martial arts, which thereby give meaning to the highest realm of martial arts.

Whether a man's martial arts reach the higher level is measured by four aspects: strength, fist position, strength and psychology. These four aspects make up an organic whole and a comprehensive embodiment of martial arts at a higher level. For a kungfu master, his force should have the quality of both pliability and hardness; his fist position should be hidden; his strength should be able to hit people by his will; and his psychology should be prepared to fight, but not act upon anger.

Being able to determine an appropriate balance between hard and soft is required for all styles of martial arts and the

The Sixth Patriarch Cutting Bamboo by Liang Kai, the Southern Song Dynasty (1127–1279)

Huineng, the sixth patriarch of Buddhism in ancient China, advocated seeing one's nature and becoming a Buddha. The drawing was drawn in bold lines in a simple, unsophisticated style.

embodiment of integrating the "internal and external" forces. Force, also refers to "yang;" and mercy means "yin." In Chinese Wushu, there is no pure hard fist position, nor a pure yielding soft fist position. If the fist is too hard, then the strength will be exhausted; if it is too soft, the strength will be too weak. Both have obvious drawbacks. Only the strength balanced between the right amount of hardness and softness can allow the fist to switch smoothly and harmoniously between the ways of yin and yang.

The phrase "cats hide their paws" derives from *Laozi*, meaning "the smartest thing seems stupid and simple." The monks use this term to explain the high-level martial arts are neither complicated nor beautiful, but practical. The beautiful thing may not be practical—and most practical things are not beautiful: this is a discipline of Wushu. That is to say, the smart one may not be better than the simple one, but most simple things can exceed the smart thing. Therefore, the mystery of Wushu does not lie within its disciplines because the smartest discipline has no discipline. "No discipline" is therefore the essence of Wushu.

Hitting others based on will means using will to introduce genuine *qi* (referring to the entire functional activities of the body), which spurs the force to hit the counterpart. This is classified in several ways: "strength comes from will," "force derives from mind" and "fist works as desired." Its principle is to transfer the energy from one's body by will power and mindset to the utmost extent, focusing one's strength to one particular point to release the great force in a flash.

Being good at fighting, without acting upon anger is a skill much needed for one to reach a superior psychological level. Laozi said that a good fighter was never angry. Therefore, a man easily angered will never be good at fighting. Thus, martial arts learners must attain a higher psychological level and be able to adjust their moods: they should be calm when they meet with enemies, remaining undaunted in the face of perils.

Thus, between hard and soft, cats hide their paws and attack using their mind while fighting, but not acting upon anger; all these combined constitute a higher level of Wushu. These four aspects are the large pillars supporting the pavilion of Wushu.

Schools of Wushu

China is a multi-national country with a long history and a vast territory. Its geographical environment and human factors are highly complex. Due to historical reasons, regional economic and cultural development is very uneven and the customs of various regions also vary, which is why a number of smaller cultural areas with distinct cultural characteristics were formed in earlier times including the Central Plains, Qi-Lu, Jing-Chu, Guan-Long, Wu Yue, Ba-Shu, Lingnan, the southern Fujian culture and the emerging cultural areas in Beijing and Shanghai. Indeed, Chinese culture has been integrated among these regional cultures.

Because Wushu is a cultural type, it is greatly affected by regional cultures. While the martial art belongs to the pure folk cultural type—its vitality lies in the hands of the upper-class. Therefore, its regional features are most profound. The major Wushu schools come from regional cultures.

Huang Zongxi, one of the foremost Chinese scholars and reformers in the early Qing dynasty (1644–1911) put forward the idea of "Neijia (internal)" and "Waijia (external)" types. He believed the type to strike the first blow and initially attack was the external type, such as Shaolinquan while the type which gains mastery by striking only after the enemy has struck was the internal type, such as the Wudangquan. Successors consider the tougher and stronger type to be the external and the gentler type to be the internal.

After a long process, Wushu has formed seven regional boxing families based on several different regional cultures. Each major boxing family focuses on one or several boxing generics, which form a number of boxing schools. The seven major

Portrait of Huang Zongxi

Huang Zongxi, also known as Huang Lizhou, put forward the concept of hitting vital points for the first time in the history of Kungfu.

boxing families are:

A: Shaolin: based on central Chinese civilization, centered on Songshan Shaolin Temple and widely distributed in the provinces of northern China.

B: Wudang: based on Jing-Chu culture, centered on Wudang Mountain in Hubei province and distributed in Hubei, Henan, Jiangsu, Sichuan and Shanghai.

C: Emei: based on Ba-shu culture, centered on Emei Mountain of Sichuan province and distributed in the provinces of southern China.

D: Nanquan: based on southern Fujian and Lingnan cultures, centered on Quanzhou and the Pearl River Delta, and distributed in the provinces of southern China.

E: Xingyiquan (intentional boxing): based on Shanxi, Yan-Zhao and Central Plains cultures, centered on Shanxi, Hebei and Henan, and distributed throughout the entire country.

F: Taijiquan: based on Central Plains and Beijing culture, centered on Henan and Beijing, and distributed throughout the entire country.

G: Baguaquan: based on Beijing culture, centered on Beijing and distributed throughout the entire country.

Shaolin, Wudang and Emei boxing families were formed earlier based on famous mountains and famous temples, and Xingyi, Taiji and Bagua were formed later, and first became popular in northern China. Martial arts practitioners like to call Wudang, Xingyi, Taiji and Bagua the "four big boxing schools of internal types."

Shaolinquan Family

In common parlance, all Kungfu from around the world comes from Shaolin. The Shaolin Temple on Mount Songshan

Songshan Shaolin Temple

at Dengfeng in Henan Province is the cradle of Shaolin Kungfu. Located in Dengfeng county of Henan province, Songshan is known as the central mountain of the Five Sacred Mountains. Located at the foot of Songshan Mountain, the Shaolin Temple is very magnificent.

According to historical records, the Shaolin Temple was built during the Northern Wei Dynasty under the reign of Emperor Taihe (AD 495). The first Indian monk to live in the Shaolin Temple was Gunabhadra (394–468). Bodhidharma (?–536), once visited the Shaolin Temple, but didn't live there for a long time. One story says he gazed at a wall in the Shaolin Monastery for nine years. Another legend said he wrote *Yi Jin Jing*. The proposition, though very influential, was eventually proved to be false, for there was a monk named BodhHiharma, but it was later found he knew absolutely nothing about the Chinese Quan.

In fact, Shaolinquan was the manifestation of the wisdom of the monks of the temple, secular Wushu masters and army generals and soldiers.

Bhadra

Bhadra was from Sindhu (India). During the Emperor of Xiaowen of the Northern Wei Dynasty, he came to China to spread Buddhism, and was respected. After the Northern Wei Dynasty relocated its capital to Luoyang, the emperor built a temple for him in Luoyang. He was fond of quietness, so the emperor built a temple for him, today's Shaolin Temple. He was the founder and the first abbot of Shaolin Temple. He translated such scriptures as Huayan, Nirvanasutra, Vimalakirti Sutra, and Ten Stages Sutra at the Scripture Translation Table. When he was old, he moved outside the Shaolin Temple until he passed away.

Bodhidharma

Bodhidharma was from south Sindhu. As a Brahman, he claimed to be 28th Zen Buddhism patriarch, the earliest Chinese patriarch of Zen Buddhism, so the Chinese Zen Buddhism is also known as Dharma Zen. He sailed to Guangzhou during the period of Emperor Wu of Liang of the Southern Dynasty. The emperor believed in Buddhism. Dharma went to Jianye, the capital of the Southern Dynasty, to meet the emperor. He talked with the emperor, but reached no agreement, so he sailed north to Luoyang, the capital of the Northern Wei. He reached Shaolin Temple, and was said to face the wall for nine years, and handed down his mantle and alms bowl to Hui Ke. In the third year (536) of Tianping period of the Eastern Wei Dynasty, he died in Luohe bank, and was buried on Mount Xiong'er.

Shaolin Kungfu originated from folk Kungfu of the Central Plains. According to archeological records, the Kungfu in the Central Plains developed at a certain level during the Eastern (206 BC–AD 25) and Western Han (25–220) Dynasties. The Qigong also accumulated rich experiences. The monks of the Shaolin Temple are mainly from the Central Plains, so some monks had already learned Kungfu before entering the temple, and they taught each other after entering the temple. The Shaolin Temple always held the tradition of widely absorbing the best Kungfu performances from the monasteries and continued to improve upon them.

At the end of the Sui Dynasty (581–618), 13 monks helped Li Shimin (599–649), emperor of the Tang Dynasty defeat Wang Shichong, popularizing Shaolin Kungfu. During the Five Dynasties Period (907–960), Shaolin Fuju invited 18 martial arts masters to help improve Shaolin martial arts. Fuju absorbed the best martial art techniques from others and compiled the *Shaolin Quan*. During the Jin and Yuan dynasties (1115–1234), Shaolin monk Jueyuan, Li Sou, a famous martial artist from Lanzhou and Bai Yufeng, a famous martial artist from Luoyang (entered the temple and took the name Qiu Yue Chan Shi) created more than 70 Shaolin martial techniques. Shaolin Kungfu gradually

Drawing of Bodhidharma sailing across a river on a stalk of reed (left) and rubbings

It is said that it was drawn by an "insane monk."

Drawing of Shaolinquan

This is the mural painting of Baiyi Hall of Songshan Shaolin Temple and also known as "Chui Pu," drawn in the early Qing Dynasty. Some movements of the painting are clear and legible and show the features of Shaolinquan.

developed and matured from the Sui and Tang dynasties to the Jin and Yuan dynasties.

Shaolin kungfu was well known in the world during the Ming and Qing dynasties. During the Jiajing period of the Ming Dynasty (1522–1566), the Shaolin Temple sent more than 80 martial monks to fight with Japanese pirates and defeated the enemies. In the 40th year of the Jiajing reign (1561), Ming general Yu Dayou (1504–1580), who was reputed for his anti-Japanese military service, went to teach cudgel-fighting skills in the Shaolin Temple. After this, Shaolin monks switched from cudgel fighting to fist fighting, so fist fights could be promoted to match cudgel fights. At the end of the Ming Dynasty, Shaolin monk Hong Ji also learned outstanding spear-fighting skills from Liu Dechang.

During the late Ming and early Qing eras, Shaolin Kungfu absorbed the best features of many northern boxing schools, the cudgel fighting skills of Fujian Province and the spear-fighting skills of Sichuan province. The broad and extensive Shaolin boxing family was formed based on Shaolin Kungfu, and finally achieved a high position in Wushu circle. At the same time, because Shaolin Kungfu became more famous, many boxing schools in northern China also claimed themselves as part of the Shaolin boxing family. In this way, the Shaolin boxing family covered nearly all the Chinese martial schools of northern region. Shaolin Kungfu became the general term for Wushu in the northern region.

Many boxing generics currently prevalent in the north such as Meihua Quan (plum blossom fist), and Paoquan (cannon fist) all belong to the Shaolin boxing family. Every type of fist has its own independent fist forms and techniques. At present, the Shaolin Temple has 371 different forms, including 234 varying types of boxing forms and 137 ways to use of weapons. There is also another saying; Shaolin has 72 types of secret arts.

Shaolinquan is known for being powerful and strong. The men from the Central Plains are tall and strong, and simple and honest, so their fists open wide and close tightly with a strong force that reveals the advantages of having long arms and legs.

Shaolinquan is simple and modest: it is based on the practicality of fighting. Their style of fist fighting is described as "fighting along a single straight line." According the method, when fighting counterparts, one should use to maximum strength to prevent his body from being attacked by his enemies. For Shaolinquan, it is required all strikes be executed within the space of a lying ox, which means the fighting distance between he and his enemies should only be a few steps apart.

The martial arts, for the most part, were shaped and cradled by the Shaolin Temple throughout history, just as Ch'an and Zen today are the result of Chinese influence. Shaolin Kungfu is therefore the "granddaddy" of all Asian martial arts. The keystone of Shaolin Kungfu is the integration of fist fighting and

Buddhism. The original aim of practicing boxing by the Shaolin monks was to protect the temple and Buddhism. Shaolin monks were required to practice meditation, which is an integral part of Buddhist practice. Dhyanna was an Indian form of Buddhist meditation, which stressed meditation by sitting and other forms of meditation to help bring about enlightenment in its practitioners. The Shaolin Temple comes out of many Kungfu masters, which have something to do with their meditation practice.

Therefore, the Shaolin boxing family has relations with six other boxing families, and also had a great influence on of the formation of Emei, Nanquan, Xingyi and Taiji.

Wudangquan Family

Another saying goes, "the Shaolin Wugong was superior in its external practice and the Wudang was internal." Shaolin and Wudang are considered the two dominant schools in the Chinese Wushu, and each are seen to have its merits.

Located in the northwestern region of Hubei province, Wudangshan stretches over 400 kilometers, covering an area of more than 30 square kilometers. The main peak, the Heavenly Pillar Peak, rises 1612 meters above sea level. The natural scenery of Wudang Mountain is powerful and magnificent. It was the Taoist Holy Land in China and a sacred mountain to Taoists.

The Taoists of Wudang Mountain began

Portrait of Zhang Sanfeng, the Ming Dynasty

This is the earliest known portrait of Zhang Sanfeng and was collected by the Li family, King Qiyang of the Ming Dynasty. Li Wenzhong, the ancestor of Li family, was a nephew of Zhu Yuanzhang and one of the founding fathers of the Ming Dynasty. It is also said that the Li family was known for its hospitality. Zhang Sanfeng visited the Li family occasionally and left the portrait.

Portrait of Zhao Kuangyin (the first emperor of the Northern Song Dynasty)

Zhao Kuangyin (927–976) was born of a general. Wudang Quan and Shaolin Quan both have the Changquan forms named after this emperor. It is said such forms were created by him.

practicing fist-fighting a long time ago. The Qing scholar Huang Zongxi believed Wudangquan was created by Zhang Sanfeng, but there is no historical record proving this to be the case. According to historical records, Zhang Sanfeng was a Taoist of the Quanzhen sect, and lived during the period of late Yuan and early Qing Dynasties. He practiced Qigong in Wudang Mountain, but he knew nothing about fist-fighting techniques.

The Wudang sect is secretive about its techniques and chooses its learners very strictly, so the Wudangquan was never widely spread. The Wudangquan was taught until the late Ming and early Qing Dynasties. In Ningbo, Zhejiang province, some Wudang martial masters such as Zhang Songxi, Ye Jinquan, Shan Sinan and Wang Zhengnan emerged. Huang Baijia (1634–?), the son of Huang Zongxi, was a student of Wang Zhengnan. It was believed Zhang Songxi taught Wudangquan in Sichuan province. At present, the widespread Songxi Neijiaquan, Wudang Neijiaquan and Zimu Nanquan in Chengdu and Nanchong, Sichuan province belongs to the Wudang boxing family. During the Guangxu period in the late Qing Dynasty (1875–1908), the Taoist successor, set up a school and taught students in Jiangning (now called Nanjing City), Jiangsu province. Therefore, Wudang Quan is still popular in

Sichuan and Jiangsu provinces. To date, Wudang Taoists still maintain the tradition of practicing martial arts.

According to rough statistics, more than 60 kinds of Wudangquan forms have been widely spread today, including Taiyi Wuxing Quan (Taiyi Five Element Form), Changquan (Long List) and Liuye Miansi palm. There are also decades of weaponry forms in the Wudang sect. The Wudang boxing family also includes the well known Xuanwu Quan, Mianzhang Quan (soft palm), Huzhua (tiger claw) Quan, Dilong Quan, Hongyuan Quan and Taijiquan.

Taoism pays attention to the state of quietness and passivity, and the passage to good health. Therefore, the Wudangquan pays equal attention to its fighting and health preserving skills. It laid claim to gaining mastery by striking only after the enemy has struck, and restricting the active by quietness.

The Wudang boxing family was formed in the late Ming and early Qing dynasties, around the same time period as the Shaolin boxing family.

Emeiquan Family

The Emeiquan family refers to the Sichuan boxing family with Mount Emei as the center. It is the second largest boxing family next to Nanquan (southern boxing) in south China.

Mount Emei stands upright in the middle of Sichuan province, tall and stretching in a never-ending line. Enriched with the spirit of the mountains and rivers in Sichuan, it is one of the most famous mountains of Chinese Buddhism. Legend says it is the ritual site of Samantabhadra.

It is said Taoists and monks on Mount Emei have a tradition of practicing martial arts, but there are only a few records in historical materials. In the mid-Ming Dynasty, Tang Shunzhi (1507–1560), a famous general who fought against Japanese

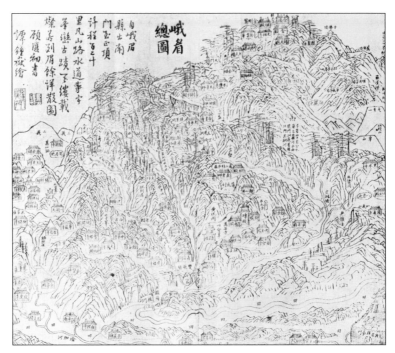

General view of Mount Emei, from *Annals of Mouth Emei* published in 1934

invaders, wrote the *Fist Song of the Emei Taoists*, which gave a vivid description of the swiftness and flexibility of the Emei fist positions. When Tang Shun promoted the Emei fist positions, the Emeiquan equipment was in the process of a qualitative leap, representative with the reputation of Emei marksmanship. The marksmanship was handed down by Pu En, a Zen master on Mountain Emei, and it promoted the development of Shaolin martial arts.

Sichuan, the land of abundance, witnessed an early developed economy and culture, and frequent exchanges with the northern part of the country. Emei fist positions took shape on the basis of a mutual exchange with local Sichuan fist positions and Shaolin martial arts. The Sengmenquan, Minghaiquan, Hongmenquan, Zimenquan, Huimenquan, and Panpomen fist positions, widely

spread in Sichuan, are said to have originated
from the Songshan Shaolin Temple.
Zhaomenquan, Shandongjiao and other
fist positions also have origin relations
with the Shaolin Temple. However,
many of these fist styles focus mainly
on Duanquan (short range boxing),
and there are obvious differences
between the Shaolin styles, which use
more fists than legs and such styles
have been localized with Sichuan
characteristics.

Among the Emeiquan family, there
are some local boxing generics, such
as Yumenquan, Baimeiquan, and
Huamenquan. There are still some rare
pictographic style boxing methods such
as Hamaquan (toad boxing), Hudiequan
(butterfly boxing), Panhuaquan and
Huangshanquan (eel boxing).

Portrait of Du Xinwu (master hand of
natural school)

Du Xinwu (1869–1953) was born in
Cili, Hunan province and graduated
from Tokyo Agriculture University. He
was an apprentice of Xu Aishi and
made great achievements.

In addition, Wudang, Nanquan,
Xingyiquan (shape-intensive fists), Taiji and Bagua families
have spread fist techniques in Sichuan. Some of them have even
evolved into the Emeiquan family.

According to recent statistics, there are altogether 67 boxing
generics in Sichuan province with 1652 set patterns, and another
276 exercises. Among the 67 boxing generics, 28 are local generics
in Sichuan, accounting for 41.79% of the total. There are 27
generics that are obviously related to the Shaolin boxing family,
or 40.30% of the total. The remaining 12 generics belong to other
boxing families.

Ba-Shu culture has always been open and assimilative, and it is
a microcosm of the Ba-Shu culture.

Nanquan Family

This is a boxing family that boasts sub-tropical oceanic atmosphere and a hills-style. With Fujian and Guangdong as the center, it is widespread in the south of the Yangtze River area, so it is called Nanquan, or southern boxing. Legend says it was derived from Fujian Nanquan, or the South Shaolin Temple in Fujian, but no strong evidence supporting it has ever been found.

Fujian folk custom was tough. As early as the mid-Ming Dynasty, Kungfu in Fujian had made a striking figure. Yu Dayou, a well-known general who fought against Japanese aggressors in Jinjiang, Fujian (today's Quanzhou), was both a fencing and wand technique master, which was rare at the time. Another master of martial arts, Qi Jiguang (1528–1588), led Qi's family forces to participate in the fighting against the Japanese aggressors, and also in the long garrison in Fujian. Qi was born in Penglai, Shandong, and his Kungfu belonged to the north Shaolin family. He taught the officers and men martial arts, and had some influence on martial arts in Fujian and Guangdong.

Nanquan is characterized by its strict regulation, compact

Gongli Quan performance by students from Guangzhou Yuanjian Girl's School, at the 11th Guangdong Games in 1930

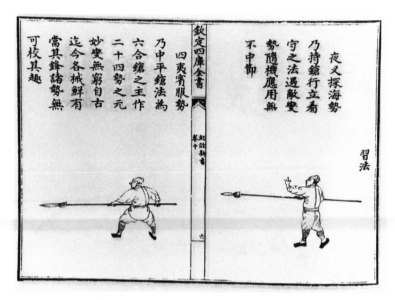

Two of 24 spear forms, from Volume Ten of *New Chronicle* by Qi Jiguang, the Ming Dynasty

action, smart techniques and lower-center movements. Southerners have relatively short arms and legs, so they pay attention to use of short fists, taking advantage of the, "better use of short instruments than long ones in special cases." Nanquan boasts mighty and quick movements, characterized by the combination of rigidity and flexibility, and arms and hand forms involve great changes. Its mighty force is fairly unique and natural.

The Nanquan family took shape in the early-to-mid-Qing Dynasty, or from the late 17th century to the late 18th century. It includes hundreds of boxing generics, and they are widely spread in Fujian, Guangdong, Hubei, Hunan, Zhejiang, as well as in Taiwan, Hong Kong and Macao. They spread to overseas communities early, and were also rooted in Southeast Asia, Oceania, and the Americas. In terms of contributing to the spread of China's martial arts, the Nanquan family is second to none.

Taijiquan Family

In Chinese martial arts, Taijiquan (shadow boxing) best displays the behavior and way of thinking of the Chinese people.

Taijiquan integrates fighting and health promotion, and is the movement of will and spirit, requiring movement guided by *Qi* and strength, showing the combination of rigidity and flexibility. Consisting of a series of spiral actions, Taijiquan is different from other boxing families; each action is in the form of a circle.

The application of such boxing techniques requires one's waist to be the axis, steadily connecting each movement, with internal strength promoting movement. Each movement seems weak, but strong intrinsically, showing the unique fighting style of attack and defense.

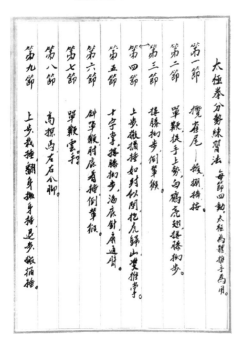

Script of separate practice method of Taijiquan by Wang Yueshan (literary name Songfeng) in Kaifeng, Henan province in 1946

Based on the attack and defense principle, Taijiquan focuses on defense, taking defense as attack, and retreating in order to advance, which is the so-called principle, "dare not be host, but be guest, dare not advance one inch, but retreat one foot," with emphasis placed on wining the strong with the weak, defeating swiftness with slowness, and conquering majority with monitory. The greatest taboo is to fight excessively. It is a kind of boxing generic that contains a profound philosophy and wisdom. It embodies the Chinese people's attitude: their understanding of life and the universe, and thus it can be called a kind

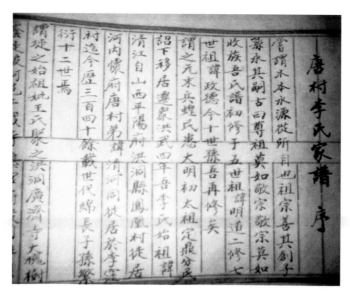

Forward of genealogy of Li Family at Tang Village in 1716 (the 55th year during the reign of Emperor Kangxi of the Qing Dynasty)

of special form of expression of traditional Chinese culture. Taijiquan is the boxing generic that boasts the greatest wisdom among internal strength boxing. However, its origin has been debated. According to the Li's family tree in the Tangcun village, Henei (Boai, in today's Henan province), modified in the 55th year (1716 AD) of Emperor Kangxi of the Qing Dynasty, and found in 2003, it can be inferred Taijiquan originated from the Qianzai Temple in Tangcun village. It was jointly founded by Li's family in Tangcun and Chen's family in Chenjiagou, Wenxian county. The specific founders were Li Zhong of Tangcun village (1598–1680), the Li Xin (Yan) (1606–1644) brothers, and Chen Wangting (about 1600–1680) of Chenjiagou, in the late Ming and early Qing dynasties. After the chaos caused by wars in the late Ming and early Qing dynasties, Taijiquan in Qianzai Temple was forced to evolve into two branches, one was Li's, and the other was Chen's.

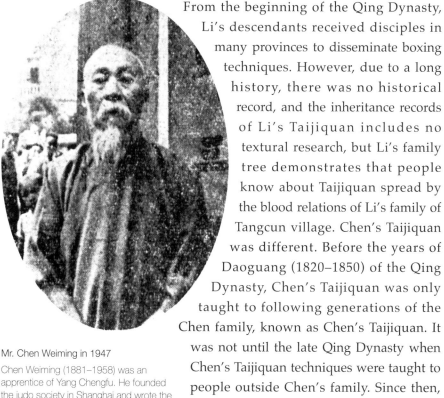

Mr. Chen Weiming in 1947

Chen Weiming (1881–1958) was an apprentice of Yang Chengfu. He founded the judo society in Shanghai and wrote the Arts of Taiji Quan.

From the beginning of the Qing Dynasty, Li's descendants received disciples in many provinces to disseminate boxing techniques. However, due to a long history, there was no historical record, and the inheritance records of Li's Taijiquan includes no textural research, but Li's family tree demonstrates that people know about Taijiquan spread by the blood relations of Li's family of Tangcun village. Chen's Taijiquan was different. Before the years of Daoguang (1820–1850) of the Qing Dynasty, Chen's Taijiquan was only taught to following generations of the Chen family, known as Chen's Taijiquan. It was not until the late Qing Dynasty when Chen's Taijiquan techniques were taught to people outside Chen's family. Since then, with Beijing as the center, it evolved into four schools: Yang, Wu, and Sun schools, which were quickly spread nationwide.

Among all the major Chinese boxing families, Taijiquan has always boasted an obvious advantage in cultural level. The works on Taijiquan witness the greatest number of in-depth theories, and are less conservative in the art of attack and defense, and fighting techniques. Again, due to the combination of fighting techniques and health promotion, it is a form suitable to people, old or young, thus making it popular around China over just several decades. It has since become the boxing family with the strongest momentum for development.

Xingyiquan Family

Xingyiquan, and Wudang, Taiji, and Baguaquan are known as the four major boxing schools of internal strength. However, its style relies on fighting and attacking, hard. Like lightning and thunder, it is unique within the internal strength boxing forms.

Emerging in the late Ming and early Qing dynasties, Xingyiquan was founded by Ji Jike (1602–1680), born in Puzhou (today's Yongji), Shanxi. It was believed Jike studied for 10 years at the Shaolin Temple in Henan during his early years, and he was especially skilled at spearing techniques. Later, he changed the spear into a fist, taking on the meaning of "mind being the initiation, and form being the destination," and thus creating Xingyiquan, which is characterized by strength and swiftness.

Years later, three schools gradually derived from Xingyiquan, with increasingly rich contents. The Shanxi school with Dai Longbang (1713–1802) as its representative, made an addendum of Wuxingquan, or Fist of the Five Elements; the Hebei school had Li Luoneng (1803–1888) as its representative. Li, born in Shenxian, Hebei province, was mainly engaged in business, and his master was Dai Wenxiong (1769–1861), the younger son of Dai Longbang. With a 10-year apprenticeship, he was known as "Shenquan Li." Li created Santi style, and he taught it to many

Portrait of Lu Songgao, master hand of Xingyi Quan

Lu Songgao (1873–1961), Hui majority, is the seventh-generation successor of Xingyi Quan by Ma Xueli of Henan and also the founder of Shanghai Xingyi Quan.

New year picture of Yue Fei seizing He Yuanqing, Tianjin, the late Qing Dynasty

Yue Fei (1103–1142) was the patriotic general of Southern Song Dynasty, famous for fighting the Jin troops. He Yuanqing fought against Yue Fei and was captured and released by Yue Fei twice. He felt ashamed and surrendered to Yue Fei to fight against Jin troops. He Yuanqing is fighting against Yue Fei in the picture. It is said that Xingyi Quan was created by Yue Fei, but this is groundless.

disciples when he returned to his native Hebei, thus establishing the Hebei school. The third school was the Henan school with Ma Xueli (1714–1790), Dai Longbang's fellow apprentice. Ma was born in Luoyang, a Hui ethnic, most of whose disciples were Hui people. In the early years of the Republic of China, the two schools of Xingyiquan in Hebei and Henan were spread to Sichuan, Anhui, and Shanghai, and then far overseas. The Shanxi school, however, was not widespread, and the final formation of Xingyiquan occurred in the late Qing Dynasty.

Xingyiquan is basically a pictographic style, whose main movements copy the predation and self-defense actions of some animals. Therefore, it is called "shape-like and mind-mimic" resembling those of a dragon, tiger, monkey, horse, alligator, chicken, snipe, swallow, snake, eagles, and bear. The movements of the Shanxi school are mainly based on 12 animals while the Hebei school focuses on 10 animals. In the actual fighting, both the Shanxi and Hebei schools use fists and palms frequently, but the

Henan school pays more attention to the functions
of the elbows, knees, shoulders and thighs.

Xingyiquan is powerful, with concise and
practical actions while it uniformly focuses on
short-term attack.

Xingyiquan also belongs to the Taoism
boxing school and focuses on internal
strength training. In the face of enemies, it
is required to mobilize the body's greatest
potential to attack enemies with sudden
strength, punching with full strength and
penetration, often imposing harm on the internal
organs of the enemies.

Portrait of Wang Xiangzhai

In the 1920s, Wang Xiangzhai (1885–1963,
disciple of Guo Yunshen), born in Shenxian county,
Hebei, discarded shapes and secured meanings on the basis of
Xingyiquan, creating Yiquan (once called Dachengquan, or boxing
of great success). The emergence of Yiquan marks a revolution in
Chinese martial arts. Wang Xiangzhai boldly gave up all routines
and repaired the tactics of traditional martial arts. Returning to
original purity and simplicity, he gave back the primary priority
needed to pile strength. Yiquan has no routines or positions. It
emphasizes on response as the situation requires. Wang once
fought with foreign master-hands on several occasions, only to
defeat the rivals with one movement.

Xingyiquan is characterized by simple actions in conformity
with actual fighting and the trend of developed martial arts.
It therefore spread rapidly. In addition, the heritors of the
Xingyiquan family in past generations were less conservative and
were also committed to theoretical research. Like the Taijiquan
family, it displays potential cultural advantages by showing great
vitality.

Baguaquan Family

Baguaquan is Baguazhang (Baguan means the Eight Diagrams in ancient Chinese culture), spread by Dong Haichuan in Beijing in the late Qing Dynasty. Dong Haichuan, born in Wen'an, Hebei, was skilled in Luohan boxing (belonging to the Shaolin boxing) in his early years. Later, he roamed around and met a Taoist in the mountains of Anhui, where he was taught Baguazhang, which promoted his techniques. When he reached his middle ages, Dong settled in Beijing and taught nearly 1,000 disciples. They benefited from Dong, and a variety of schools quickly evolved. They included: Yin's Baguazhang spread by Yin Fu (1840–1909). Yin

Fu was a professional master of martial arts; Cheng's Baguazhang spread by Cheng Tinghua (1848–1900). Cheng Tinghua ran a glasses shop in Beijing known as "Glasses Cheng" when the Eight-Power Allied Forces invaded China, he was shot dead by the German army; Song's Baguazhang 1 was spread by Song Changrong; and Song's Baguazhang 2 was spread by Song Yongxiang; Liang's Baguazhang was spread by Liang Zhenpu (1863–1934), who formally acknowledged Dong Haichuan as his master at the age of 14.

When Baguazhang spread to the second generation, it had evolved into five branches: Yin, Cheng, Song (two branches), and Liang. Therefore, in the late Qing Dynasty and early period of the Republic of China, the Baguaquan family took shape initially with Beijing as the center.

Portrait of Dong Haichuan

In the first year of Guangxu in the Qing Dynasty, Guo Yunshen (1855–1932), renowned master of Xingyiquan, came to Beijing out of admiration, negotiating with Dong Haichuan

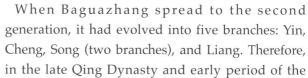

Portrait of Fu Zhensong holding the eight diagrams broadsword in 1929

Fu Zhensong (1881–1953) was an apprentice of Jia Qishan (apprentice of Dong Haichuan). In 1928, he served as the master of Baguaquan at Central Guoshu Academy. He learned from others' strong points and founded Fu-style Taijiquan, which is popular both at home and abroad, especially in the United States, Canada, Brazil and Southeast Asia.

on the integration of Xingyiquan with Baguazhang. Later, Zhang Zhankui (1864–1948) followed Dong Haichuan to learn Baguazhang, and followed Liu Qilan to learn Xingyiquan of the Hebei school, and gradually combined both schools into one, creating Xingyi Baguazhang. At present, it is still spread in Sichuan and Shanghai.

Baguazhang used palms instead of fists, with steps in the form of circle, which broke the traditional fist positions and steps in straight line, opening a new arena for Chinese Wushu. Its step positions focus on lifting, trampling, swaying, knocking, rotating around and maintaining continuity.

Weapons

As for the "18 kinds of feats" mentioned in ancient China, they refer to the use of 18 varieties of weapons. The argument has always been different, but generally refers to a bow, crossbow, spear, stick, knife, sword, lance, shield, ax, tomahawk, halberd, pole, whip, mace, hammer, fork, harrow and dagger-axe. Indeed, there are more than 18 varieties of weapons in ancient China, and moreover, the weapons used in martial arts are quite different from those used in military operations. People who do martial arts pay attention to individual fighting while military operations focus on group efforts and unity.

There are strange weapons in martial arts, and all kinds of hidden weapons, with the total number reaching as many as 100 varieties, many of which have not been handed down from past generations and are on the verge of extinction as a result. In recent years, the most

Weapon room, stone relief of the Han Dynasty, unearthed from Nanyang, Henan province

The weapon room contains a spear, lance, bow and shield. The figure near the bottom is the patron saint.

Bronze Yue of the Warring States Period

Yue, a kind of weapon, is a bronze axe with a long handle. The axe is flat and sharp with strong penetrating power. Yue looks like an axe and is bigger than an axe.

Ge

Ge is a special weapon used in ancient China with a handle and was used for hooking, picking and cutting. Ge has a chiseled edge, forward cutting edge and vertical handle. Its internal edge is used for hooking and cutting, its external edge for pushing and poking, and its forward cutting edge for picking. In ancient times, Ge and Gan went under the general name of "Gange," a common name for all weapons.

commonly used weapons in martial arts are knives, swords, spears, sticks and whips.

Short Weapons

The so-called short weapons refer to the light weapons that are less than the length of a normal eyebrow, and are often held with a single hand in practice. The most common short weapons are a knife and sword.

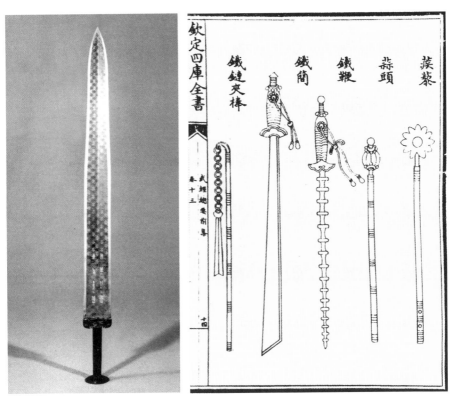

Sword of King Goujian of Yue State, late Spring and Autumn Period, unearthed from Jiangling, Hubei province.

It is 55.6 cm long and 4.6 cm wide with a Chinese inscription, which means "King Goujian's Sword" in English. It is still very sharp and dazzlingly brilliant and is known as the masterpiece of swords of the Wu and Yue states.

Short weapons of the Song Dynasty

This series of knives includes a single knife and double knives; both are used mainly for cleaving and chopping. A single knife requires swiftness and bravery while double knives boast better appreciation value. A master uses double knives just like he would rolling balls.

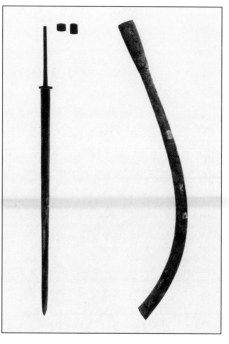

A sword has a double-edge, mainly used for stabbing. It falls into two kinds, namely, a single sword and a double-sword. Single swords account for a big proportion. Some swords are furnished with sword tassel (also known as the sword gown), which are literal swords, and those without tassels are called military swords.

Bian Jing sword (left) and Wugou, the Qin Dynasty, unearthed from Lintong, Shaanxi province

The Bian Jing sword has a flat stem and is so sharp that it can cut 18 pieces of paper at one time. It was still sparkling when unearthed. After assay, it is covered with an oxide layer of chromium compounds to prevent rusting.
Wugou is 66 cm long and has double blades. It can be used for pushing and hooking. The unearthed weapon supports evidence for the records of historical documents.

The ax is also a kind of short weapon today. But axes used in ancient warfare had long handles, commonly known as "broadax," which belonged to the category of long weapons.

There are two kinds of whips, namely soft and hard. A hard whip is made of steel and consists of 13 sections. The most commonly known is a bamboo-like steel whip with a sharp end, which is mainly used for hacking and smashing and can also be used for picking and punching. A soft whip is known as a 9-section whip, consisting of 9 sections of thin steel or cooper rods. Its length is slightly shorter than the height of a person, and its movements are mainly winding and brandish in the form of a circle.

Mace is a long strip of steel weapon, usually having four edges without blades, or no sharp ends. With a length of about 0.8m, it also belongs to a kind of weapon for hacking and smashing. There are also double maces, each are about 0.6–0.7 m long.

A hook is a kind of multi-blade weapon with a blade on its body while its end is hook-shaped. An armguard is crescent-shaped with a sharp point and blade.

Canes are a kind of wooden weapon, divided into short and long. A short cane is about 0.7 m long, and a long cane is about 1.3 m. It is characterized by the horizontal handle near the end of the crabstick in the form of a "T." It is used not only for striking and smashing, but also for hooking and pulling away the weapons of rivals. A stick is close to a cane, but the horizontal handle of the stick is at the far end of the crabstick, also in the shape of a "T." The stick is about 1.2 m long and can be used with one or two hands.

A whip-stick is a short wooden rod, about 1.3 m long and slightly thin. It is said to have originated from a horsewhip stick. It is short without an edge, portable and easy to use, and quite popular in northwestern China. There is also a short weapon from ancient times called an iron ruler, which is about 0.6 m in length, slim and long without sharp points and a blade. It is mainly used for hacking, smashing, pointing, and punching. Once popular in the Qing Dynasty, it is now extremely rare.

Long Weapons

The most common weapons in martial arts are spears, sticks and falchions.

In martial arts, the spear is known as "the king of weapons."

Xu Ning imparting usage of brush-hook spear, an illustration of Chapter 56 of *Outlaws of the Marsh*

A brush-hook spear is a kind of spear with an overhead hook on the blade of the spear head. According to *Tales of the Marshes*, the marshes prevailed against the armored cavalry of the Song troops.

As the saying goes, "a spear thrusts in a line." Requiring a straight line in practice, there is a saying that believes the middle horizontal thrust is the chief of a spear, which is hard to defend. It relies mainly on an outward block, followed by an inward block and then a thrust.

A stick has the longest history out of the long weapons. It is called "shu" (ancient shu had an edge without a blade), and covers a wide variety. If classified by shape, there are long sticks, eyebrow-level sticks, shaozi sticks and many others varieties. If classified by materials, there are wooden and iron sticks. The wooden stick is the most common. Primary stick techniques are quick and powerful and mostly including spinning. With a large attack space, it is believed, "a stick can hit a lot of rivals."

Three-section stick consists of three sections of hard wood connected by iron hoops, which can be used flexibly. A shaozi

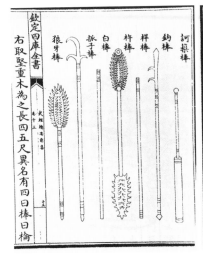

Clubs of the Song Dynasty

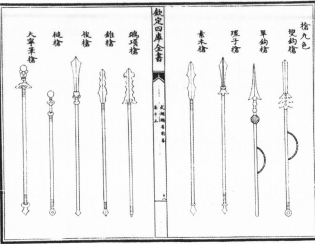

Long spears of the Song Dynasty

stick is connected by a short, hard piece of wood at the end of the stick with iron hoops, which can unexpectedly and effectively help users when fighting against enemies.

A falchion is fitted with a long handle, and is also known as a "spring and autumn falchion," "yanyue dao (reclining moon falchion)," or "long falchion." During the Tang Dynasty (618–907), falchions were 3 m in length and weighed 7.5 kg. With blades on both sides, it was called "Mo Dao." Today, falchions used in martial arts have blades on one side. There is another kind of "po" broadsword, whose handle is shorter than that of a falchion. It is long and narrow, and used with both hands.

There are also some other kinds of long weapons. The "ji," or halberd was popular before the Northern and Southern Dynasties and included a long-handled single halberd and short-handled double halberds. The latter is a kind of short weapon. The long-handled single halberd is divided into two types: fangtian ji, with two crescents on the right and left sides of the end, and qinglong ji, with a crescent on one side.

The fork is a common weapon, mostly used by hunters in ancient times, and includes the ox horn folk and "three-head fork" or "triangle fork," commonly known as the "tiger fork." Fork techniques derive from those of the spear, and can also be used for locking and seizing weapons of rivals.

The shovel is a rare weapon, first used by farmers as a weeding tool. Both ends of the shovel are furnished with blades. The front end is meniscus-shaped, concave inside with the meniscus facing outward; the tail is an ox-shaped handle with a blade at the end. Legend has it the shovel is a kind of Buddhist weapon, also known as "fangbian shovel" or " meniscus shovel." The application of the shovel looks light and has unique

Sword-shaped halbert, the mid-to-late Warring States Period, collected in Nanyang Museum

It is special in shape and is a rare sharp weapon.

Chinese officials with their attendants in the late Qing Dynasty
They are holding bamboo staves, three-point steel forks and broadswords.

fighting techniques, which include pushing, pressing, patting, supporting, rolling, shoveling, cutting and picking.

The rake is a weapon that also evolved from a farming tool. The rake with nine teeth at the end of it is called an iron rake, and is as sharp as a nail. It is about 2.4 m in length and weighs 2.5 kg. It can be used for smacking, or for defense.

The tang, a kind of fork-like weapon, is a rare weapon. It has a sharp point in the middle of the end, which is called the front edge and is about 0.5 m long. The rear has an outward crescent on which a row of sharp blades are inlaid. The tang handle is up to 2.5 m in length and has an edge-shaped iron drill called the "zun."

Hidden Weapons (*anqi*)

Hidden weapons refer to projectiles, or weapons used for a quiet hit by stealth. The Chinese Wushu went into its heyday in the Qing Dynasty. In the latter of the dynasty, the firearm became increasingly popular and hidden weapons gradually became outdated. However, some Wushu learners still use such techniques today.

The hidden weapons are divided into four categories, including thrown weapons, rope-like weapons, shooting weapons and poisonous projectiles. Each category consists of several types of weapons.

The thrown

Gold-decorated bronze trigger-mechanism of a crossbow, the Western Han Dynasty, unearthed from Linzi, Shangdong province

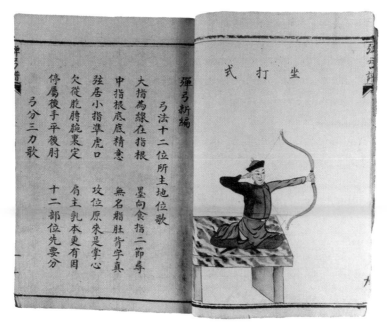

Book of Spring Bow, published in 1806 (the 10th year under the reign of Emperor Xianfeng of the Qing Dynasty), collected in Capital Library of China

weapons include flying pikes, darts, flying forks, flying sabers and plum-blossom needles.

The rope-like weapons consist of rope darts and meteor hammers.

The shooting weapons include sleeve-hidden arrows (arrows hidden in a sleeve), catapults and regular arrows.

The poisonous projectiles consist of sleeve-hidden cannons (small cannons hidden in a sleeve), sprays and a beak-shaped pistol.

Some hidden weapons, including blow arrows, daggers and gimlets, cannot be classified within the four categories.

The thrown weapons are the most popular and diversified among all the hidden weapons. Darts, also called hand-hidden darts, they come in trigonal, pentagonal and cylindrical shapes with pointed ends in the front. The darts are around 10 cm in

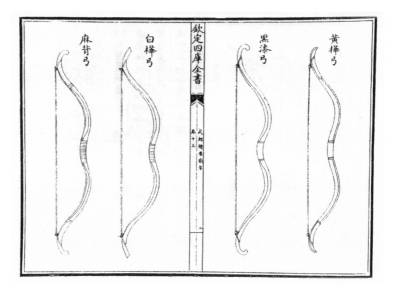

Bows of the Song Dynasty

length and weigh 0.2 kg. The darts usually have a stripe of red or green silk tied on to the end, called the "dart coat," which is around 8 cm in length and helps the darts fly steadily.

The flying forks are made of iron and have three tips in front, with the longer one in the middle and the other two cutting-edge tips on the outsides. The three tips are sharp and in the shape of a spearhead. The flying forks are around 27 cm in length and weigh between 0.25 to 0.5 kg. The fork handle tapers off from the back end to the front.

The plum-blossom needles are also a common type of hidden weaponry. The plum-blossom needles are composed of five steel needles with back ends connected together. The needles are around 3 cm in length. Once the needles make contact, they produce five wounds in the shape of plum blossom, hence its name.

The rope darts, meteor hammers, flying claw and soft whip are most popular among the rope-like weapons.

Arrowheads, bronze weapons of the Warring States period, collected by Tianjin Baocheng Museum Garden

The rope darts refer to a steel dart tied with a long piece of rope at the end. The steel darts are a little bigger than the normal darts, around 0.2 m in length and weighing 0.3 kg. It has a pointed tip and its wide end is circular in shape. An iron hoop at the end of the dart is used to tie the rope, which is around 6.7 to 10 m in length.

Steel lotus, a kind of weapon

Making crossbow, an illustration from *Tian Gong Kai Wu*

Tian Gong Kai Wu was an encyclopedia of technology with illustrations by Song Yingxing (1587–1661), a writer-scientist of the Ming Dynasty. It collected many manufacturing technologies of weapons of that time.

The meteor hammer is composed of an iron hammer and a long rope. The iron hammers are usually in the shape of a ball, paw or gengon. It weighss around 1.5 to 2.5 kg.

The sleeve-hidden arrows are the most popular among the shooting weapons. They include the single-tube arrows and the plum-blossom-tube arrows. Both kinds of weapons tie to the lower arm with the front of the tube close to the wrist. The tube is designed with springs and a special mechanism. One arrow can be installed and shot from the single-tube. However, the plum-blossom-tube contains six small arrows, one in the middle and the others around it, which takes the shape of a plum-blossom, and can be shot continuously. The arrow's stem is made of a thin bamboo around 20 cm in length. The stem has an iron head at the front end. The single-tube is around 24 cm in length and its 2.4

cm-diameter is made of bronze and iron. A small hole at the top of the tube is used to install arrows, which are shot from a small hole at the front end of the tube. The plum-blossom-tube is thicker and has a 3.5 cm-diameter and is 24 cm long.

The catapults are also very common among the shooting weapons. They are made of hard wood and designed with a pod used to install an arrow stem. The crossbow is designed at the back end of the catapult and is controlled

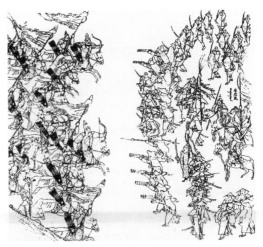

Counterwork between Ming and later Jin troops from *Qing Shi Lu*

The Ming troops used firearms with broadswords, whingers and lances (on the right), while the later Jin troops still used bows and arrows at war.

by the catapult body. The catapults are very small and usually around 33 cm long.

The sleeve-hidden cannons are the most popular among the poisonous projectiles. It is a special hidden weapon featured by intermixing gunpowder. It is educed from the muzzle-loading cannons of the past. It is made of bamboo pipe, which size is similar to that of a small handless wine cup. The pipe is around 40 cm long and has three iron hoops on the outside. Both ends of the pipe are wrapped with a thin iron coat; one end is the mouth of the cannon mouth, while the other is used to load the gunpowder.

Three Stages of Chinese Wushu Practice

After thousand of years of growth, Chinese
Wushu has developed into many schools
of thoughts and each school has its own
special practice methods and techniques. As a
knowledge system, though classified into several
categories and schools, all Chinese Wushu
follow similar practice methods. According to
the common disciplines of Chinese Wushu, the
Kungfu exercises can be divided into three stages
or levels, including refining spirit into qi (visible
strength), qi into vitality (invisible strength), and
vitality into void (refined strength). Refining
the spirit into qi refers to the primary stage
and attaches great importance to exercising
basic techniques, eliminating excess tension
and developing strong strength. Refining qi
into vitality is the intermediate stage and gives
profound attention to eliminating strong strength,
cultivating soft strength and nurturing internal

Monument of Wushu practices, the
Qing Dynasty, unearthed at Mount
Yuexiu in Guangzhou

force by Xingyiquan. Refining vitality into void refers to the senior
stage and gives great importance to exercising extreme soft strength
and accessing the supreme level of combined boxing and morality.

The Wushu learners repeat the basic techniques to gradually
eliminate the excess tension and cultivate the strong strength during
the primary stage.

The basic technique is the introduction to Kungfu and consists
of stance, footwork, arm, waist, finger and eye exercises. After
mastering the basic techniques, one can start quan (boxing), which
is the actual beginning of the primary stage. The basic technique
exercises are regarded only as the preparation work for this stage.

Refining the spirit into qi aims to refine strength. One who does
not use his natural strength in Wushu fighting uses his raw power
or excess tension. Such strength will fade away with the aging

Quan Jing from Volume 14 of *New Chronicle* by Qi Jiguang, the Ming Dynasty
Created by Qi Jiguang, it is a simple style and practical.

of physiological functions and does not belong to the strength of Wushu. The strength of Wushu refers to the immediate explosive power that relies on physical coordination generated by the soul on his waist. Such power is strong and fast—and can hit objects as suddenly as a flash of lightning.

The immediate explosive power is the burst of strength from key joints of the human body, including the shoulders, elbows, wrist, crotch and knees. Strength from whichever joint belongs to the resultant strength of the human body on the basis of the synchronous cooperation of joints and instantaneous explosion of power. Visible strength can be produced without preparation when the practice reaches a certain degree. The Wushu learner can generate great power by joint movements in limited space, and such power is commonly referred to as *cunjin* (explosive strength).

To resolve problems in the primary stage, one must learn Chaiquan (splitting set exercises). Chaiquan means to split the offensive and defensive movements from the set exercises and study the functions and usage of the movements in real combat. Chaiquan is one of the key trainings in technique exercises.

After learning the basic techniques and several set exercises, one can learn Chaiquan to practice several actions, which lays a firm foundation in hand, footwork, eye and body exercises. Simultaneously, one can gather the *qi* scattered in the body in *dantian* to eliminate the excess tension and grow strong strength. Once the excess tension is eliminated completely, the body will be full of strong strength, spirit and vitality. The body then becomes strong, and the steps steady. The visible strength has been achieved, while the exercises benefiting the bones are completed. This brings one to reach the level of refining spirit into *qi*.

People who complete the primary stage are usually strong and vigorous, and have sharp eyes. Sometimes, they are hot-blooded, unyielding, impetuous and proud of their martial art techniques. If they pursue further study to enter a senior level, such characteristics can be refined.

Refining *qi* into vitality refers to the intermediate stage, where one completes the exercises to benefit the muscles and grow invisible strength. Invisible strength refers to soft strength. However, "soft" in Wushu doesn't mean "weak," but "flexible." The invisible strength integrates soft and strong strengths, which supplement each other. The stage of refining *qi* into vitality is meant to eliminate strong strength and grow soft strength. This stage is the second period of strength improvement.

Refining *qi* is key to this stage. In fact, one shall learn to gather the *qi* scattered in the body in *dantian* during the primary stage of refining the spirit into *qi*, during which one cannot control the flow of genuine *qi* (zhenqi).

After years of exercise to help improve the internal organs, the strong strength gradually fades away, and the soft strength grows and the congenital *qi* (yuanqi) thrives. Those who harness invisible strength are often clear-minded and full of energy. If they encounter a difficulty, they could react very soberly and rarely respond with their hands or fists.

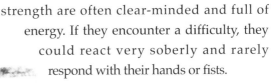

Li Jinglin performing Taiji Jian in 1930

Li Jinglin (1885–1931) was the vice curator of Central Guoshu Academy at that time.

One who completes years of hard exercises for invisible strength will have a further understanding on the extensive and profound martial art techniques. Such individuals are often found to be easy-going and lacking in arrogance as a result; they also do not show off their martial art techniques, nor bully others. When the exercises, which benefit the muscles, are completed, one will also notice improvements in figure and looks. Firstly, the figure becomes increasingly thin and healthy, with no troubles of obesity. Secondly, one can walk with a spring in their step, without a reel or a stagger. Thirdly, the eyes become as sharp as lightening when fighting against the enemy, but at other times the eyes remain clear and affable. When one has no such violent looks, the person has reached the stage of refining *qi* into vitality.

Refining vitality into void is the senior stage of both Wushu and exercises meant to benefit the internal organs. One shall complete the exercises to benefit marrow and gain refined strength. The invisible strength will be developed through the refined strength after reaching the state of extreme soft strength and flexible power. The higher level of strength does not exclude the Wushu movements and techniques for attack and defense.

Refining vitality into void is the most senior levels of training for the central nervous system and reaction capacity of the human body. According to the traditional Chinese Qigong theory, the stage of refining vitality into void shall be done at the upper *dantian*, a round range close to "muddy pellet" (*niwan gong*); the stage of refining *qi* into vitality shall be done at the middle *dantian*, a round range in the rear of *zhongwan* and *jiuwei* plexus; the stage of refining spirit into *qi* shall be down at the lower *dantian*, a round range a round range under the belly button. The exercise ranges are gradually raised from the bottom-up. The key to refining vitality into void is to achieve "void" and "quiet." The void refers to the modest inner center, while quiet refers to the normal mood.

Wushu masters who reach the level of refining vitality into void are often generous, courteous and open-minded people. One who completes the exercises of refined strength can be called a Wushu master, who is gentle, elegant and appears free from worry. These masters have clear eyes, and their eyebrows come to a healthy red sheen in the middle, which is a sign of brilliant achievement in Wushu. However, such an accomplishment is difficult to achieve.

Yi Lu Hua Quan transcribed by the author of this book at Kaifeng, Henan province in 1971

If an intelligent person begins to learn Chinese Wushu at 10-years-old without any interruption under the guidance of a famous Wushu master in a sound environment, it takes somewhere around 20 years for this person to complete the long journey of the three stages. That means a real Wushu master is at least over the age of 30. And sometimes, the journey can take even longer. Doing exercises to benefit the internal organs is also related to age, experiences and cultural awareness of the learners. Generally speaking, middle-aged individuals are better able to understand the true essence of Wushu and complete the long journey of Wushu exercises from the easy to difficult and complicated stages. Therefore, those who gain great achievements in Wushu shall be over 40 years old.

Characteristics of Chinese Wushu

As the offspring of the history and culture of the Chinese nation, Chinese Wushu holds the special internal features and temperaments of the Chinese nation. Chinese Wushu has its own national characteristics, which differ from foreign combat techniques.

Systematic

Among the historical and cultural heritages of the Chinese nation, Wushu is a large and complete system. Compared to other cultural heritages, it has relative independence.

The Chinese Wushu has many schools. Almost all Wushu schools take the *Yin* and *Yang* and Five Element Theory as the common basis of philosophy and regard "harmony between soma and spirit" and "harmony between quan and dao" as the end result of Wushu exercises. In view of the theories on quan techniques, Chinese Wushu develops complementary to Confucianism, Buddhism and Taoism. The exercises which benefit the internal organs mainly borrow ideas from traditional

Shaolin Monks Practicing Wushu in the Mountains

Chinese medicine and the Taoist practices of maintaining good health. Therefore, Chinese Wushu combines the philosophy, medicine, the art of attack and defense, and practice of maintaining good health, to make up one large and profound theoretical system. This makes the martial art unique around the world.

Other internationally popular combat techniques are characterized by speed and strong movements. But despite their respective theories, such combat techniques lack discussion on connotation; the theories only focus on the external movements of the attack and defense movements. Some combat techniques used in Muay Thai only have simple forms and no set exercises. It has speed and strong movements, but no devotion to deep theories reflecting the psychological features of Southeast Asian peoples. Karate from Japan evolves from the Shaolinquan of China, reflecting the Yamato characteristics of perseverance, emulousness, valor and discipline. Boxing reflects the psychological features of Occidental peoples, including enjoying exercises and pursuing stimulation. By contrast, Chinese Wushu is characterized by the profound connotations, the gentle manners, the harmony of dynamic and static movements and the integration of strong and soft strength. Such characteristics are part of the psychological features of the Chinese nation.

Strict Order

Regardless of the schools, there are strict rules to practicing Wushu. Wushu learners must follow certain orders; there are no shortcuts. Most schools teach the course from the basic techniques; quan and weapon techniques are exercises meant to benefit the internal organs. It first begins with a series of external-internal exercises, a process of macro-micro level techniques, which are followed by internal-external exercises, a process of micro-macro level techniques, which completes the course. At this stage, learners are able to integrate body and spirit, and obtain internal and external harmony.

The strict orders of Chinese Wushu are based on the combination of ancient combat techniques and the Taoist methods of maintaining good health, which is unique in the world. However, there are some similarities among the strength-based Muay Thai and boxing, which are equivalent to the strong strength of Chinese Wushu. Although Japanese Karate contains exercises which benefit the internal organs, it still gives top priority to strong strength. Because both Muay Thai and Japanese Karate focus on the actual combat, they are inferior to the strict orders of Chinese Wushu.

Principle of Gradualness

The principle of gradualness is another feature of Chinese Wushu. This requires a lot of patience and persistence to learn. The course only can be completed gradually and is impossible to succeed quickly. Because Chinese Wushu places high demand on the basic techniques and attaches great importance to the rudiments, the actual combat techniques are seldom passed to the beginners. And because Chinese Wushu regards the exercises which benefit the internal organs to be the foundation, and pays great attention to the practices of maintaining good health (nurturing qi) and moral cultivation (setting moral values), the combat techniques have never been put first. Such combat techniques are quite different from those of the foreign combat techniques.

Unlike Chinese Wushu combat, Muay Thai, Japanese Karate and boxing all aim to destroy the object. Though they have their basic techniques, the actual combat exercises are taught after the basic techniques are learned. This enables beginners to master some combat techniques quickly. People learning Muay Thai can participate in a Wushu contest on stage after five years of three-stage exercises including basic exercises, single movement practice and simulated combat practice. However, five years only allows the strong strength to be practiced, which is the primary stage of Chinese Wushu. If a Muay Thai learner and a Chinese marital arts learner fight each other after five years of exercises, the latter will likely be unable to withstand the fierce attack of the former. If the combat is held after ten years of practice, the latter is unlikely to be defeated. If the combat is held after 15 years of exercises, the latter will surely be the successor. This is because the foreign combat techniques mainly depend on strong strength and are too eager to attain quick success and instant benefits. While some Muay Thai boxers make their fortune from the techniques, their strength is quickly sapped after they reach the age of 30. Meanwhile, many Muay Thai boxers endure injuries during combat, which are hard to relieve due to the focus on strong strength and lack of exercises to benefit the internal organs. Therefore, longevity in the foreign boxer and Muay Thai boxer is rare. As for the Japanese Sumotori, they usually only live about forty years, similar to the Muay Thai boxer.

The principle of gradualness determines the long journey of progress when beginners learn combat techniques. Because Chinese Wushu combines the practice of maintaining good health, the martial art can help practitioners lead a longer life. As long as the learners keep practicing the exercises year after year, they can master enough of the actual combat techniques needed to prolong life. Such gradualness can also be seen clearly in age. Foreign boxers usually reach their prime between the ages of 20 and 30. However, Chinese Wushu masters often mature after the age of 30. Some reach a zenith around the age of 40, and their signature techniques marking their fame remain unchanged even into their sixties and seventies, or longer.

Nurturing *qi* and Moral Cultivation

Chinese Wushu regards moral cultivation as its foundation. It advocates nurturing *qi*, integrating law and promotes both civil and military ability, going against aggression and violence. Many Wushu masters regard the practice as a means of moral cultivation and health maintenance. The Chinese Wushu circles always give top priority to Wushu ethics. Every Wushu school has established strict regulations. Any one who does evil or harm, regardless of their martial art techniques is unwelcome among the Wushu circles. Various schools in the Wushu circle also admonish their followers not to fight with others, cause trouble, or bully others ignorant of Wushu. They advocate helping others for a just cause, wiping out bullies and helping the downtrodden.

Chinese Wushu regards the exercises to benefit the internal organs as its foundation, and base exercises on nurturing *qi*. Nurturing *qi* aims to reach taihe (grand peace), which is impartial and combines softness and firmness. The *qi* of grand peace runs in the opposite direction against the emulative thoughts. *Qi* is harmonious with rationality, while quan is harmonious with law. The more prosperous the *qi* is, the weaker the emulative thoughts becomes. The more achievements made by the Wushu learner, the better the

King of Yiyong Wu'an, ink drawing in the Song and Yuan dynasties, collected by Russian St. Peterburg Museum.

Guan Yu is the embodiment of humaneness, righteousness and braveness. In 1123 (the fifth year under the reign of Emperor Xuanhe of the Northern Song Dynasty), Guan Yu was conferred the title of "King of Yiyong Wu'an."

New year picture: Zhao Yun fighting in Changbanpo, mid-Qing Dynasty, Yangliuqing, Tianjin
Zhao Yun was a famous general of the Shu state during the Three Kingdom period.
According to the picture, Zhao Yun is surrounded at the center with princekin in his arms
fighting with Caocao's troops. The picture in color of black and blue is for use of families after
funerals.

temperament of the Wushu practitioner becomes; Wushu learners
rarely show off their powers. Moral cultivation and nurturing *qi*
are the unique guiding concepts of Chinese Wushu.

Aesthetics

Most set exercises and movements of Chinese Wushu have an
aesthetic feeling, which lies in the attack and defense movements.
The set exercises combine the dynamic and static movements.
They are highly diversified and characterized by unique rhythmic

sensation and beauty. Chinese Wushu displays the movements and shifts under certain time-space conditions by vigor strength and quick speed. Moreover, the set exercises are difficult and can show the courageous and enterprising spirits of mankind. Aesthetically, Chinese Wushu is diversified. The quan techniques of Piguaquan, Bajiquan, Chaquan and Huaquan are quick-paced, elegant and full of masculinity. Meanwhile, Shequan (snake boxing) uses movements that wriggle like a snake and are full of femininity. The Baguazhang and Taijiquan combine its dynamic with static movements, softness with firmness, and the beauty of masculinity and femininity. Its aesthetics styles are diversified and full of aesthetic feeling. No other combat techniques can be

Film star Lu Cuilan performing a sword dance at Nanjing winter disaster relief meeting in 1930

Swordsmanship performance by
Luan Xiuyun from Qingdao in 1934

compared to taiji.

Fundamentally, the aesthetic value is contradictory to the combat function. Many practical movements of Chinese Wushu lack aesthetic value. Over the development of more than 2,000 years of Chinese Wushu, it has experienced a simple to complex progression, followed by a complex to simple state. Chinese Wushu was simple and never used to have so many schools and *quan* families. But a number of schools of martial arts thrived and diversified during the Song, Yuan and Ming dynasties. Wushu entered its golden age in the early Qing Dynasty. Some Neijiaquan (internal martial arts) such as Taijiquan, Xingyiquan and Baguaquan emerged in the late Ming dynasty. Neijiaquan allows a smaller force to defeat a larger one, and also enables simplicity to replace the complex. Its contents and set exercises later become concise and practical. Such trends also appear in the development of many schools of Waijiaquan. It reflects the law of development of Chinese Wushu. The combat function is always first in Wushu, which defines the trends of Wushu development.

The aesthetic value is always secondary and occupies a subordinate position.

In a word, Chinese Wushu is unique and one of the most natural forms of traditional Chinese culture. Any form of foreign combat techniques bears no comparison with it. Chinese Wushu has made its presence on the world combat stage with its unique combat techniques and practice methods. The truth verifies that Chinese Wushu hails in no comparison to any other combat technique in the world.

Chinese Wushu and
Chinese Culture

Wushu, a collection of thousands of years of human wisdom, embodies the national traditional culture in martial art form and also reflects the self-defense and health practices of Chinese people. The core philosophy of Wushu is drawn from the Confucius principle of physical and mental integration combined with neutralization; the Taoist principle of dynamic balance; the Buddhist principle of showing cultural syncretism of Confucianism, Daoism and Buddhism in China; and the Eastern theory, which believes man is an integral part of nature.

Compared with other Chinese cultural forms, martial arts are seen as a highly exclusive cultural system. With the exception of the Buddhism practices introduced during the Han and Wei dynasties (202 BC–AD 265), Wushu was hardly affected by external influences. Martial arts were essentially derived from the lower class, which reflects the character, thinking patterns and behaviors of China's ancient lower class. Therefore, martial arts should belong to a purely civilian cultural class. Against "elegant cultures" such as music, chess, calligraphy, painting and poetry, martial arts appear hard and rough. At the same time, though Wushu maintains the simple and unsophisticated appearance of the country, it is characterized for its robust beauty and is still considered as a piece of pure land in the field of Chinese traditional culture.

Wushu and Regimen

Chinese Wushu highlights the harmonization between soma and spirit, and combines the inner and outer qualities. By nurturing a good temperament that fills one with vigor and vitality, and offering exercises to help lead a longer life, Wushu has long been considered as an effective way to maintain good health. And while it is also credited with helping to build a strong immune system to fend off sickness, keeping an aging body in good spirits, some still question whether this is true.

Good physical fitness differs from a prolonged life, despite their links. There are many facts that prove longevity is a complex issue which involves a wide range of factors. Practicing Wushu or Qigong is just one of the factors associated to living a long life, but they are not the only ones.

Wushu may keep one fit

It is widely known practicing Wushu may help build a stronger body, but maintaining physical fitness is seen as more of an outer appearance. Therefore, Wushu's role of maintaining good health is reflected more in the exercise it offers for the central nervous system and inner organs. According to the ancient Chinese regimen, "essence, energy and spirit" were the three key elements to living well. Here, the "essence" refers to the original essence that comes from the kidneys and is fundamental to human life, known as "Mingmen" (not Mingmen point). "Energy" refers to the original vigor that is innate and rests in the kidneys. Meantime, the "spirit" refers to the fact that human nature and true minds are the outer reflection of "energy."

"Essence, energy and spirit" are all provided at birth, but are later reduced and damaged by various emotions and desires

Portrait of Yan Yuan

Yan Yuan (1635–1704) was a famous scholar of the early Qing Dynasty and one of the few versed in both civil and military affairs. He advocated practical use and was opposed to boasting talk and founded the Yan Li School. He was good at martial arts and internal work. The portrait was unearthed in Taiyuan, Shanxi province in the early years of the Republic of China.

Martial arts team of Henan Preparatory School for studying in Europe and America
(1912–1921), Kaifeng, Henan province

that come successively in later days. This leads to weakened
vitality, all sorts of diseases, extreme tiredness, premature aging
and a shortened life. The Taoism Culture of Health Preservation
in ancient China stressed the need for humans to develop innate
energy with acquired energy to help restore essence, energy and
spirit to its original state, helping achieve perfect integration and
harmony between humans and the nature.

Some consider the practice of Taiji to be capable of improving
the physical fitness of human bodies both inside and outside,
balancing Yin and Yang, and allowing for energy and blood to
flow more smoothly, to prevent high blood pressure and many
chronic diseases. For example, the Nine Palace & Eight Trigram
Palm is believed to renew the cell membrane, enhance body
immunity and prevent cancer diseases. The Taiyi Wuxing Quan is
said to help balance the functions of internal organs, keep blood
lipids down, increase lung and heart performances, improve
blood circulation and thus prevent coronary heart diseases. Taiji
boxing, so long as it is practiced continuously and correctly, is

Photo of Yang Chengfu (1883–1936) performing Taiji Quan

also associated with helping to build strong bodies. Moreover, the combination of Taiji exercise and energy circulation are said to bring overall benefits to human health.

Chinese Wushu also includes many health preservation practices, and the "stake skill for better health" in the Xingyi Boxing is a case in point. The stake skill, based on the principles of "making both body and mind relaxed," makes the practitioner mentally silent and focused through a combination of still or slow, gentle motions. The process regulates the excited central nervous system and removes the chaos and tiredness in human brains while activating the physiological functions of various human systems, improving internal organ performances and thus, keeps one fit both physically and mentally. Xingyi stake skills include dragon-like Kungfu, tiger-like Kungfu, ape-like Kungfu, bear-like Kungfu and health regulation Kungfu, which are suitable for the old, weak or those with chronic diseases.

A Wushu master who has been cultivated both internally and externally, and has both superb martial skills and morals, will always maintain their peace of mind, and will neither be corrupted by wealth, nor shaken by horror or dishonor. They will never seek power and wealth, nor will they be upset about gains or losses in life, or flaunt their martial art skills. The role

Photo of Pu Yi practicing quan, in the early years of the Republic of China, collected by the Palace Museum

Qing Dynasty won the country on horse. So, the imperial family of the Qing Dynasty placed emphasis on archery, horsemanship and martial arts. Even the dethroned emperor Pu Yi (1906–1967) also practiced quan at the Imperial Palace.

of Wushu in health preservation can be best displayed in such Wushu masters. Wushu, therefore, nourishes and purifies the spirit. Physical fitness is just an outer form of effect from the practice, while a peaceful mind and the power to master oneself represent the inner fitness in the most important sense, which is the essence of Wushu as a tool for maintaining good health.

Following the law of nature is the key to longevity

Due to the number of elderly people with silver hair who have practiced Wushu all their life are vigorous and walk at a brisk pace, it has been proven Wushu leads to longevity. Wushu practicing indeed helps prevent disease and prolongs human life, but begs the question: how many seniors over the age of 100 practice Wushu?

There are some Wushu practitioners who have lived for 90 years and longer among the superb Wushu masters, such as Yang Yuting (1887–1982) who practiced Taiji, Ma Meihu (1805–1924) and Liu Wanyi (1820–1918) who practiced Xingyi Boxing, Zhang Zhan'ao (1817–1916) and Wang Ziping (1881–1973, who practiced spring kicks. Still, despite the existence of many long-time Wushu practitioners, the life span of some modern Wushu masters were not that lengthy, and those who practice the same kind of Wushu may not necessarily lead the same length of life. The Taiji master Wu Tunan (1884–1989) died at the age of 105, while Yang Chengfu, Li Yishe (1832–1892) and Chen Zhaokui (1928–1981), who were also Taiji practitioners lived only for 50 to 60 years. Of course, human longevity depends on multiple factors like inheritance, economic situations, living conditions and psychological qualities, but such cases also reveal that

Ning jiaokuan, a 96-year-old Taoist, performing shooting arrows, Shandong Guoshu Examination in 1934

practicing Wushu is not the only precondition of longevity, and does not necessarily bring about a prolonged life.

Mastering basic skills and turning brute force into physical latent force is the first step to learning Wushu. Beginners must practice everyday all year round regardless of rain or snow. But, those who learn Xingyi boxing risk injury to their legs and feet if they use too much force, and these injuries are often overlooked when young, instead affecting the Wushu master as they age. Moreover, certain kinds of Kungfu skills, such as stake kicking Kungfu, iron head Kungfu and iron arm Kungfu, are more prone to causing permanent damage to the bones and muscles of beginners who are young, aggressive and eager for success. Outer injuries, therefore, are likely to occur when practicing obvious force.

When it comes to practicing potential force and neutralizing force, internal energy based and masculine energy is gradually weakened. Internal energy cultivation mainly requires individual contemplation and guidance of thought more than communication with other fellows. Masters generally teach their pupils more routine skills and less internal energy. Therefore, many Wushu practitioners typically develop their internal energy little by little, and in the exploration process, detours and deviations are quite common.

Internal energy cultivation involves quiet and clean surroundings apart from the concentrated spirit of the individual. Unexpected shock can easily scatter their energy, or even disturb the meridian system, resulting in mental confusion or partial paralysis known as "going crazy and out of control." When practicing the potential force or neutralizing force, therefore, inner injuries are more likely to occur from incorrect practice methods or accidents. Learning Zhoutian Kungfu can cause dizziness, or even high blood pressure, if too much force is involved.

Portrait of Buddist Arhat in Red by Zhang Daqian in 1944

Wushu masters also feature aggressive dispositions and like to compete with each other. Many practitioners traveled through Jianghu after learning real Kungfu and made friends with others by rivaling in Wushu. The so-called "making friends through Wushu" refers to making a lot of friends by competing against on another. But injuries are common during competition since both parties regard each other as the deadly enemy and are fighting for survival. Therefore, one has to compete with others numerous times before earning prestigious as a Wushu master.

Generally speaking, Wushu masters have a strong sense of

winning and losing, and have developed the concept of "defeating others with superior Wushu skills" from the moment they start learning Wushu. Affected by such ideas, Wushu masters are usually on alert and are ready to compete with others at any time and any place. This also teaches them to be sharp. The psychology of being alert at all times ensures the Wushu masters are in a constant state of nervousness, which allows them to develop into an intangible spiritual pressure that modern medical science believes is harmful and contributes to cardiovascular disease or cancer.

In summation, Wushu masters do not necessarily enjoy a longer life due to the discussed physical and mental reasons, and practicing Wushu does not necessarily result in longevity. Nearly nine out of 10 seniors around the age of 100 are not Wushu practitioners. But, many of them also live in pollution-free villages, where the air is fresh,It not only allows elders to be open-minded and shielded from world strife, but also enables them to lead a thrifty life without unhealthy hobbies like smoking or drinking, or over stress of physical labor, which are the reasons for their longevity.

Portrait of Zazen

About Qigong

Qigong is also called "Neigong" or "Lianqi" in the vocabulary of Chinese Wushu. The term "Qigong" first appeared at the end of the Qing Dynasty, and was called

Zen Buddhism

Zen Buddhism, one of the 13 sects of the Chinese Buddhism, was said to start from Bodhidharma, and prevailed from the sixth patriarch Hui Neng. After the mid and late Tang Dynasty, it became the mainstream of the Chinese Buddhism, and also one of the most important symbols of the Chinese Buddhism.

Zen Buddhism does not require a special cultivation environment. It focuses on a certain luck to become eminent by chance and acquire the realm of clear mind. However, the realm of clear mind requires not "access to sacredness from commonness" but "access to commonness from sacredness." Zen Buddhism upholds that cultivation does not require one to read scriptures, or become a monk or nun. One can live ordinary daily life as usual. The daily life of those who succeeded in Zen Buddhism cultivation has no difference from that of ordinary people, and the difference lies only in the state of mind. There is only a momentary slip between ordinary people and Buddha.

Zen Buddhism has created many new meditation methods such as roaming. All the methods can enable people to have the sensitivity to immediate enlightenment. The enlightenment is beyond all time and space, cause and effect, and past and future, and obtains a sense of freedom to be free from all things and all constraints, thereby overcoming the material desire and attaining sainthood, and freeing from rigid adherence to the worldly things, but still living a normal daily life.

"Xingqi" or "Daoyin" in ancient times. Based on the meridian theory, it is a form of maintaining health using respiration regulation and "qi" circulation as the major method. Qigong is regarded as one of the most traditional Chinese regimens.

Traditional Chinese culture can be considered a combination of Confucianism, Buddhism and Taoism. As a minor branch of the traditional Chinese culture, Qigong also falls into three categories: the Confucian, Buddhist and Taoist styles. Among them, both the Confucian and Taoist styles took shape very early, while the Buddhist-style Qigong was introduced to China along with the Buddhism.

Confucian-style qigong is characterized by "seated meditation," with "quiet sitting" as the main form. The Taoism qigong, guided by *Zhou Yi (the Changes of the Zhou)* and the theory of Yin-Yang and Five Elements, boasts a long history, rich literature and the greatest influence. Given that *Zhou Yi* is the classic work of Confucianism, the Confucian and Taoist styles can be said to have essentially originated from the same source, affecting each other and penetrating one another. However, Confucian qigong is more influenced by the Taoist style in its evolving process while Taoist qigong incorporates the effort and offers the richest written works.

Buddhist qigong also includes many sub-branches, with the most influential ones being Jingtuzong, Chanzong, Tiantaizong and Mizong.

Chanzong (Zen Buddhism) has been the most popular one among all the Chinese Buddhist braches since the Tang Dynasty and is followed by Jingtuzong. Chanzong and Jingtuzong merged into one called the "combined practice of Chanzong and Jingtuzong" after the Song Dynasty. Meanwhile, Jingtuzong advocates pursuing the western pure land of happiness, gaining popularity among ordinary people; Chanzong highlights the power of understanding and thus influences the intellectuals most. Chanzong qigong takes "Chanding" and comprehension as its major forms and "zuogong" (also called "zuochan") is the most common practice. From Tiantai Mountain located in Zhejiang, Tiantaizong advocates Zhiguan Famen, which is used to guide qigong practice. "Quiet sitting" is its major form, which focuses on the sense of *qi*, accompanied by self-developed gong.

Mizong, also called Tantra Yoga, was introduced to China from India as early as the Three Kingdoms Period, and spread in to Chang'an (currently Xi'an) and Luoyang areas in the Tang Dynasty, and later exported to Japan where it was developed into the Japanese Zhenyanzong style. It almost disappeared following the "Huichang Suppression of Buddhism" in the late Tang

Portrait of Dao Yin (restored), the Western Han Dynasty, unearthed in Changsha, Hunan province
The portrait had 44 figures of men and women with brief explanatory notes. Its contents consisted of treatment and healthcare.

 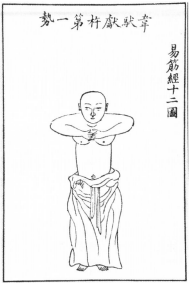

The first picture of *Shi San Duan Jin*, from *Internal Work Illustration* published in the eighth year under the reign of Emperor Xianfeng of the Qing Dynasty (1858).

The first formation of *Yi Jin Jing*, from *Internal Work Illustration* published in the eighth year under the reign of Emperor Xianfeng of the Qing Dynasty (1858).

Dynasty and the turbulent Five Dynasties Period, but was carried forward in Tibet and evolved into several branches. Mizong is closely associated to the ancient Indian Yoga, its spread, however, is only limited to the Tibet area, but people on the inner land did not learn it until the 1930s and 40s.

In a zigzag-spreading process, Confucian, Buddhist and Taoist styles have all been integrated with each other over a long period of time, affecting and complementing each other.

Qigong is regarded as a science, but historical reasons inevitably bring a touch of religious and sorcery elements into it. Regimen and qigong have intricate and undeniable links in China, and Neigong in Wushu is connected to Qigong, too. Qigong must be mentioned here as the issue of Wushu and regimen is being addressed.

The origin and development of Qigong had a closed relationship with self-aggrandizement.

Since early times, human beings dreamt about a kind of supernatural ability overwhelming all restriction. That was because, in reality, they had been dominated by the laws of nature and had been tortured frequently by nature. Therefore, they relied on this kind of delusion to deal with the weakness and passiveness. Thinking about the myths, they were thought to be the way the early people challenged nature and the cosmos in the delusion.

Later, with the development of society, human beings became more mature,so their delusions began to diminish. However, the self-aggrandizement of human did not disappear, but deposited deep in the soul, turning into a kind of unconsciousness to be passed down from generation to generation.

In fact, because humans do not enjoy being alone, they always challenge nature. After many failures, they still continue seeking new targets. Finally, they find the targets—themselves, which are available at all times and mind no responsibility for potential risk.

Few humans and the powerful and changeable nature make up the contradiction between the two parties with great disparity in strength. It seems that human do nothing to their strong opponents, but yet want to challenge their physiological limits. Two thousand years ago in the East, Chinese Taoists began to recognize and develop their physical power under the help of many health preserving methods, while Indians did so under the help of Yoga. The result of their development was what we call Qigong today.

When developing the physical power, our primogenitors found that, by exercising Qigong, even common people were able to have some kind of unimaginable power. For instance, Qigong can make the muscles of the body as tight as iron and with prodigious resistance to external attack. This kind of Qigong is called "Jinzhongzhao" or "Tiebushan" in martial arts. It can make the bodies of people softer so that they can bend and stretch their bodies flexibly, and this is called "Tongzigong" in martial arts. It can also make people more powerful, so that they can break stones and bricks using their hands and cut off stone monuments with their feet, which is called Yinggong in martial arts. In addition, Qigong can help prevent diseases and maintain health, which enables them to live a long and healthy life, and this kind of Qigong is called Yangshenggong.

In the psychedelic and wonderful Qigong, self-aggrandizement concealed deep inside human hearts can be aroused. Human beings want to surpass themselves, their lives and time, and they are willing to break away from all the restrictions. Therefore, their delusions get excited when exercising Qigong.

Life is what human beings value the most. Chinese people have profound understanding on this point so that they are more dedicated to developing health preserving methods than Westerners.

In accordance with the traditional Qigong theories, in order to exercise Qigong well, a person should first maintain a clear heart and conscious, meaning no desire for fame and fortune, being quiet, good endurance, determination, tolerance to loneliness and insight. With these preconditions, the person may succeed.

Qigong is helpful for preserving health. However, the result of the exercises may be different if exaggerated.

Wushu and Literatures, Films and TV

Wushu is a quintessence of China, which is closely connected with Wushu and Chinese people's knight-errant complex. Over two thousand years, from the Pre-Qin period to the Republic of China era, there have been numerous legends about knight-errant, and history abounds in many examples of this kind. Therefore, Xia Culture, developed from Xia people (a person adept in Wushu and given to chivalrous conduct), was specially developed. The core of the culture is the sagas of the knight-errants, while the knight-errant complex is the psychosocial basis of this culture.

Most people like reading swordsmen novels. However, they tend not to focus on the inconceivable Kungfu, but the charm of personalities, such as braveness and magnanimousness, courage and determination, promises that cannot be counted on and self-sacrifice. Under the pens of the authors, the knight-errants with swords travel around on an unrestricted base. They break the bondage of mundane regulations and laws—and never bend to nobility. They dare to reveal corrupt officials. Often, they live in the mountains and ancient temples, or appear in restau-

Woodcut of Shui Hu Ye Zi: Song Jiang and Shi Jin by Chen Hongshou in the late Ming Dynasty

Chivalrous complex of the Chinese people

Chivalrous complex falls basically into the scope of folk culture. It is ordinary people's imaginary resistance against the prevailing order, and also longing for perfect heroic character. The so-called "where there is injustice, there will be an outcry." Social injustice is the root cause of the violations by force, and the historical root of the chivalrous complex of the Chinese people. As is described in the Water Margin, "The Buddhist monk's staff cleared the dangerous road, and Buddhist monk's knife removed all the injustice." The chivalrous complex of the Chinese people also contains a persistent psychological prayer that is the longing for that tremendous personality power. Cultural history research shows that in the historical development process of a nation, a kind of mass character that the nation lacks most usually becomes the lasting spiritual pursuit of quite a few individuals of the nation. In China, the most desired is a healthy and complete personality free from servility and obsequiousness.

rants, where they hold big feasts and drink and spend money recklessly. There are beautiful ladies and nice wines. The cold swords contrast with the light the moon. They fight hard against adversity and destiny. They never show their love, or enmity. They live a magnanimous life and choose to die solemnly. The authors show the real degage lives to the readers.

The knight-errant complex can be reflected in poems and operas. For example, excellent Kungfu and errantry have been mentioned in the *White Horse* (*Baima Pian*) by Cao Zhi (192–232), *Knight-errant on Travel* (*Xiake Xing*) by Li Bai (701–762), *Farewell to Liang Huang* (*Bie Liang Huang*) by Li Qi (690–751(indeterminate)) and *A tale of a Girl from Lanling* (*Lanling Nüer Xing*) by Jin He (1818–1885) later in the Qing Dynasty. These works have been widely read. Tracing back to the 20th Century, when films and TV programs were being developed, many characters of these swordsmen novels began to appear on-screen.

It should be noted that swordsmen novels do not reflect the reality of the life, but rather the fantasy world. They present a world that common people dream about and what ordinary people want in their hearts. In China, these novels may become the permanent fairy tales of the nation while the knight-errant complex has been integrated into the historical psychological accumulation of the nation as a special element of Wushu. Therefore, it is seen as a permanent retrospection in the history of the development of the internal spirit of the Chinese nation.

New-style swordsmen novels

Louis Cha (Jin Yong, 1924–present) brings new vitality and perfection to Chinese swordsmen novels. Therefore, masculinity and gentleness become two new characteristics of Chinese literature works. It means Chinese swordsmen novels have entered a new era.

It seems to be a historical opportunity. In the 1950s, due to political reasons, swordsmen novels disappeared rapidly on the Chinese mainland. Meantime, some famous authors also disappeared from the literature world. However, it was at that time, Louis Cha became a success in Hong Kong, and made his way to the top among the other swordsmen authors.

Except Louis Cha, the authors who wrote swordsmen novels during the period also included Liang Yusheng, Gu Long (Xiong Yaohua), Dongfang Bai and Wolongsheng (Niu Heting) in

Hunting drawing of Emperor Xuande, the Ming Dynasty
The drawing illustrated Emperor Xuande (1426–1435) in garments of the Tartars as he went hunting at the countryside.

Hong Kong and Taiwan. These authors and Xiao Yi, an overseas Chinese in the United States, made up a new author group, and their novels were called the "new-type swordsmen novels."

The new-type swordsmen novels are recognized as fairy tales for both adults and children. On the basis of inheriting the artistic traditions of the existing excellent works, the new-type novels focus on bringing out the inner spirit of human beings and creating vivid characters with distinctive personalities. The characters created in these works usually have the emotions and desires of common people, but at the same time, each of them are endowed with some kind of superb Kungfu skill, which makes them seem god-like. Therefore, these novels tend to be fiction novels. The new-type novels also integrate characteristics of both fairy tales and myths. In this sense, the new-type novels lead a new path into the literature world.

The new-type swordsmen novels, in fact, are combinations of romantic novels and swordsmen novels. They formally talk about Wushu, but actually talk about emotions. Meanwhile, these novels are written by referring to the techniques used in Western literatures and films for expression. In these novels, emotions are highlighted, while Wushu is indulgently exaggerated upon.

Each author has a special artistic pursuit, so their works are of different styles. Among these authors, Louis Cha, Liang Yusheng and Gu Long are the most distinguished and influential. At least a hundred million people on the Chinese mainland have read the works of Louis Cha, and there are few Chinese who are unfamiliar with this man.

The charm of Louis Cha's novels comes from the author's understanding of life, his deep insight to history, well-arranged plots and unique writing style. His choice of words and plot are basic skills that ensure the high quality of work by any author. However, without a deep understanding of life and insight to history, the work lacks vigor of life and profound history.

Procession of Emperor Qianlong with Fragrant Imperial Concubine by Giuseppe
Castiglione of the Qing Dynasty

Giuseppe Castiglione (1688–1766), Italian, came to China to preach his religion in 1715 and
served as the imperial painter and a left many paintings. *The Book and The Sword*, written
by Louis Cha, has mentioned the story between Emperor Qianlong and Fragrant Imperial
Concubine.

The works of Louis Cha often surround a theme of conflict
between personality and destiny. The characters in his books
pursue two states of perfection: the perfection of Wushu and
life. And nearly all of them attain a good understanding on life
during the process of pursuing the perfection of Wushu. As a
result, their splendid lives become more admirable under the foil
of their excellent Kungfu. The novels of Louis Cha are also seen
as historical records of the characters, which document how they
grow up to be mature, how they exercise Kungfu and what they
experience in their lives. Louis Cha is also known for creating
tragic atmospheres, where his characters grow up and experience

Cosmic iron sword, August, 2004, Beijing

Cosmic iron refers to iron from cloud stone and also known as "Xuan Tie" in ancient times. In fact, it is permenorm alloy. In Gaocheng of Heibei province, a bronze Yue with iron blaze made by cosmic iron was unearthed, which belonged to the mid-Shang Dynasty. The sword in picture is made in recent years and is 100 cm long and weighs four kilograms. The sword is sparkling and sharp with special patterns of cosmic iron. In *the Return of the Condor Heroes* by Louis Cha, Yang Guo used such a cosmic iron sword.

many difficulties. Many of these characters, such as Xiao Feng, Zhang Wuji, Hu Fei, Yang Guo, Chen Jialuo, Yuan Chengzhi and Di Yun, have lives with irreparable regret with unrealized aspirations. They often do not have the chance to put their excellent skills to use.

Heroes are born from tragedies. How many heroes have come forth through the history of war for the Chinese nation? Louis Cha understands the rules of history. He concentrates on the tragedies of history in his books and his characters shoulder the heavy loads of both history and their lives, which highlights their personalities.

But the use of emotion is what really draws the readers in, allowing them to resonate with the characters in the story.

Wushu is similar to the art and philosophy under the pen of Louis Cha. For example, the Baihuacuoquan of Chen Jialuo in *The Book and the Sword*, Tangshi Jianfa in *A Deadly Secret*, Shufaquan of Zhang Sanfeng in *The Heavenly Sword and the Dragon Saber*, Luoyingshenjian Zhang of Huang Yaoshi in *The Legend of Condor Heroes* and Anranxiaohun Zhang of Yang Guo in *The Return of the Condor Heroes* are all sublimed Wushu that are similar to the arts and lack no philosophical speculation. While other authors pale in comparison to Louis Cha, there are a few that must be mentioned when discussing Wushu literature.

Liang Yusheng (1924–2009) has 40 works, the most outstanding one of which is *Ping Zong Xia Ying, Romance of the White Haired Maiden* and *Heroes of the Tang Dynasty*. His works are full of literary characteristics. Most of them are classically elegant, and consist of excellent artistic conceptions and descriptions of women in these works. But some of Liang's works lack authenticity while others are excessive and lack appeal.

Gu Long (1936–1985) leads another way. He references many Western whodunits and uses a lot of montage skills adopted from films. Therefore, his works are "westernized" and

Nan Jiyun from China's Scenery by Okada Gyokuzan published in AD 1802.

Nan Jiyun was born in Dunqiu (today's Xun County of Henan) in the Tang Dynasty and was good at archery. He resisted the troops of An Lushan, then was captured after the county fell into the enemy, and finally died.

cater to the interests of young people. Gu Long has more than 80 works, including *Handsome Siblings*, *The Sentimental Swordsman*, *Chu Liuxiang* and *The Legend of Lu Xiaofeng*. The characteristics of Gu Long's works include modern and sharp words, mysterious style, more cool tones than warm tones, and more sorrow than pleasure. In his works, there are speculations on the philosophic theories of life, profound conclusions on life experience, wonderful profiles of lives and vivid characters. However, carelessness and negligence are reflected in his works, resulting in overall mediocrity, where peals and stones, sagaciousness and superficiality coexist in the same works. The works of Gu Long are weird, but that also spurs his success. However, the characters in his works lack improvement and the proper connotations of history and life.

Gu Long led a miserable life. For a long time, he lived alone and drank heavily. He died in his forties. It is said that Li Xunhuan, the famous "Xiao Li Fei Dao"—a character in *The Sentimental Swordsman*, who also lives a lonely life and drinks everyday—is the epitome of the life of the author himself.

Action Film and TV

In the 1960s, knight-errant film became popular in Hong Kong. Famous action star Bruce Lee (Li Xiaolong) (1940–1973) conquered people of all colors. Thanks to him, people all over the world knew "Chinese Kungfu."

Bruce Lee was a master in Kungfu. His original name was Li Zhenfan, and Xiaolong was his stage name. At age of 13, he

Film still from *Burning Honglian Temple* (1928–1930) Film still of Wu Lizhu from *Guan Dong Da Xia* (1930)

Photo of performers and clerks from Shanghai Mingxing Company (1934)

Xia Peizhen (1908–1975) (the first one on the front row from the right), Hu Die (the third one on the front row from the right), the director Zhang Shichuan (1889–1953) (in the middle of the back row)

Movie Queen Hu Die (1908–1989) in 1933

became a student of Ye Wen, a Hong Kong master in Yongchunquan, and then went on to become a student of Shao Hansheng to learn Luohanquan and Tanglangquan. At age 18, he went to the United States to study philosophy at Washington State University. In 1965, he established the first school of Chinese Kungfu in the US. In 1967, he named the Wushu he created "Jeet Kune Do," which made Chinese Kungfu schools more complete.

In 1971, Bruce Lee became famous overnight by playing a leading role in

Huang Liushuang (1907–1961, the first one), the famous Chinese-born actress performing martial arts at Hollywood in 1930

Huang Liushuang, whose ancestral home was Taishan of Guangdong province, was born in Los Angeles. She became famous overnight by acting as a Mongolian bondmaid in the *Thief of Baghdad*. She came back to China many times for shooting movies.

the film named *The Big Boss*. He then played the lead actor in the *Fist of Fury*, before taking a role in *The Way of Dragon* and *Enter the Dragon*. But, in both films, he not only acted, but also directed. On July 20, 1973, Bruce Lee died suddenly while filming the *Game of Death*. He died in acute brain edema and was buried at a memorial park in Seattle.

Bruce Lee played the roles of heroes who were masters at Kungfu dedicated to safeguarding the dignity of the Chinese nation. In each film, Bruce displayed his excellent Kungfu skills. *The Way of Dragon* included the most wonderful action shots of his films. This film has been made into an introduction film for learning Jeet Kune Do. In addition, it provides an example of competition between Chinese Kungfu and Karate.

Five years later after the death of Bruce Lee, Jackie Chan (Cheng Long) became widely famous in Hong Kong.

Film still of Bruce Lee from *Way of the Dragon* in 1973

Jackie Chan was originally named Chen Gangsheng. He was born in 1954 in Hong Kong though his ancestral home is Shandong. Because he lived a poor life when he was young, he was sent to the Peking Opera School run by Master Yu Jim Yuen. Ten years later, he became a master in Kungfu. At the age of 17, he became a stunt man and acted in Bruce Lee's films. After that, he changed his name to Chen Yuanlong, and then to Cheng Long in 1976.

In 1978, Jackie Chan played the leading roles in the *Eagles Shadow* and *Drunken Master*, but he did not gain much success from these films. However in 1985, Jackie Chan directed the film *Police Story*, consolidating his dominance as an action star. Jackie Chan then went to Hollywood and became popular for his role in *Rumble in the Bronx*. Later, he directed *Rush Hour* and the *Highbinders*, becoming the most popular Chinese star with the highest box office value in Hollywood.

Film still of Jackie Chan from *the Medallion* in 1982

After the success of Jackie Chan, Jet Li (Li Lianjie), another man from the Chinese mainland, rose to action movie stardom.

Jet Li is a Beijinger. He started to learn Kungfu when he young. From 1974 to 1978, he topped five consecutive National Wushu Championships and participated in performances abroad several times. In 1982, when he was 19, he played the leading role in the film *The Shaolin Temple*,

Film poster of Shaolin Temple in 1981

which was backed by Chung Yuen Motion Picture Co. The film, made on the Chinese mainland, included a number of national Wushu champions, and demonstrated the real Kungfu of China, surprising the world soon after its release. It set record box office returns in Hong Kong and was widely popular in both Asian and Western countries. It directly raised the enthusiasm for learning Chinese Kungfu around the world. The film essentially paved the road to fame and Hollywood for Jet Li.

In 1983, action films *Wulin Zhi* and *The Undaunted Wudang* were produced on the Chinese mainland. The leading actor of the former one was Wu Bin, then coach of the Beijing Wushu Team, and the leading actor of the latter one was Zhao Changjun, a national Wushu champion. Both films were instantaneously popular.

In 2000, the film *Crouching Tiger, Hidden Dragon,* directed by Ang Lee, caused a huge international response, creating a martial arts film craze across the world. The film is based on the story of the same name written by Wang Du Lu. Ang Lee incorporated in

Hong Kong film director Lau Kar Leung directing actors during movie making in the 1970s

Lau Kar Leung is a famous martial artist, action director and film director. He takes the real martial art route after Bruce Lee and is also the first film director from action director. The left photo illustrates Lau Kar Leung directing John Chiang mantis boxing, while the right one shows him teaching Chia Hui Liu to use three-jointed pike.

the film the essence of Kungfu film and literary film, interpreting Chinese classical aesthetic tradition and emotional concepts from a new perspective. The film won many awards at international film festivals, and got the 73rd Oscar for Best Foreign Language Film, gaining the highest international reputation in the history of Kungfu films. In addition, the film also had spectacular box office success, hitting more than $200 million global box office revenues, the highest among the Chinese-language films ever. After that, *Hero,* directed by Zhang Yimou, and *Kungfu,* composed, directed, and starred by Stephen Chow, also met with great success, with a global box office hitting more than $100 million.

As for the popularization of TV action series, Hong Kong played a major role. Many Louis Cha novels were adapted and made into TV series shows. The most popular TV series shows produced on the Chinese mainland include the *Swordsmen, The Demi-Gods and Semi-Devils* (*Eightfold Path of the Heavenly Dragon*). All of these were met with a high audience rating. In fact, nearly all the actors played in these series were Kungfu laymen. But the popularity of these TV series did not last long. Because most of the actions were performed using stunt skills, the series lacked authenticity—a common weakness of TV action series. Meanwhile, other adapted works took quite a different approach to the characters and plots compared to the books, diluting the historical and cultural connotations of the original works. Poor actors and actresses also further diminished the attraction of the TV series shows.

Chinese and Foreign Wushu Exchange

Chinese Wushu has been improved and integrated during cruel competition. It faced many tests against other exotic martial arts. In history, Chinese Wushu confronted two major challenges. The first one happened in the 16th century during the Ming Dynasty when Samurais invaded China. The second one happened in the early 20th century, when the opponents included both Samurais and Western boxers. Chinese Kungfu masters won the challengers at last, but not without recognizing the advantages of other styles of fighting and the deficiencies of Chinese Kungfu.

Since the 1980s, Chinese Wushu eventually became more internationally popular, became the first target for competitors of the world fight circle. Chinese Wushu has experienced three other challenges. The first challenge was anti-invasion, and the second challenge was revenge on the "Sick Man of East Asia." The third challenge came in the form of athletic competition on the basis of fighting fairly and politely. For the third challenge, Wushu lost no burden of history and has embraced competitive sport.

Two Big Challenges in the Martial History

Two major challenges to the Chinese martial art came from foreign fighting; one occurred in the middle of the Ming Dynasty, and the other in the early 20th century.

During the Jiajing Period of the Ming Dynasty (1522–1566), a large number of Japanese samurai, known as *Wokou* (Japanese pirates), invaded the Southeast area of China. These Japanese samurai were fierce and merciless. They colluded with Chinese pirates to attack and encroach Chinese prefectures and counties, burning, killing and looting wherever they went in Jiangsu, Zhejiang, Fujian and Guangdong provinces. Over a hundred years, the government of the Ming Dynasty moved out its armed forces to defeat the Japanese pirates.

The Japanese samurai are accustomed to using *Wodao* (long knife), which is slender and heavy with a thick back, and thin and cocked edge. Qi Jiguang, a Chinese military general and national hero during the Ming Dynasty, found that Chinese soldier knife skills were poorer than the Japanese samurai, so he trained his soldiers to use *langxian* (a utensil made of bamboo brush), big stick, long lance and other long weapons to fight against the Japanese *Wodao,* and made outstanding achievements in fighting against the Japanese pirates. This demonstrated the

Sword of Qi Jiguang's troops

Portrait of Qi Jiguang

Drawing of battle array (partial), the Ming Dynasty

Chinese swordsmanship set was no better than that of Japan during the mid-Ming Dynasty. While Qi Jiguang defeated Japanese pirates while the military fought, competition between the Shaolin monks and Japanese samurai is argued to be the most direct competition between Chinese and Japanese Kungfu.

According to the historical records, in 1553 (the 32nd year of the Jiajing era), Japanese pirates began a large-scale invasion of Nanhui (belonging to Shanghai today). The Shaolin monks led the fight and utterly defeated the Japanese pirates. The Shaolin monks defeated the Japanese pirates many times, and more than 30 monks sacrificed their lives for the country.

More importantly, the Shaolin Kungfu defeated the long knife of the Japanese pirates, and taught the Japanese samurai, who consider themselves a world above others, the toughness of Chinese Kung Fu, creating proud records for Chinese Wushu history.

More than 300 years later, China and other foreign countries carried out another big battle at the end of the 19th century, which lasted nearly half a century, ending in the 1940s. The battle location began in Beijing before moving to Tianjin, Shanghai and then Tokyo. It was the true competition between the Chinese masters and foreign masters. After the fights were over, the label on old China, "Sick Man of East Asia," was consigned to the dustbin of history. The Chinese Wushu circle shared the same hatred for the common enemy and wrote a song of moral sense for Chinese Kungfu.

According to statistics, the major fighting examples at that time included:

Che Yonghong (1833–1914, Xingyiquan style),defeated a Japanese samurai in 1888 in Tianjin; Huo Yuanjia (1869–1910, Mizongquan), scared the British giant away in Shanghai in 1910,before defeating four people from the Japanese Judo Association in Shanghai; Han Muxia (1867–1947, Xingyiquan style), won a fight against Russian strongman Kang Tyre in1918 in Beijing; Wang Ziping (1881–1973, legs and fists), defeated Russian strongman Kang Tyre in 1918 in Beijing, American strongman Alaman and Germany strongman in 1919 in Qingdao, before defeating Japanese Sato in 1919 in Jinan;

Chen Zizheng (1878–1933, eagle claw boxing), beat an American boxer in 1919 in Shanghai, and a British boxer in 1922 in Singapore; Sun Lutang (1861–1932, Taijiquan), defeated a Japanese samurai in 1922 in Beijing, and six Japanese samurai in 1930 in Shanghai; Tong Zhongyi (1879–1963, Liuhe boxing), beat a Japanese samurai in 1925 in Shanghai;

Yang Fawu (no details for date of birth, wrestling technique), gained a series of victories of three Japanese judo masters in 1930 in Tokyo;

Ji Wanshan (1903–?, Shaolin boxing), won a Russian strongman in 1933 in Harbin; Ma Jinbiao (1881–1973, Cha Quan), defeated an

American man in the 1930s in Nanjing; Wang Xiangzhai (1885–1963, Yi Quan), defeated Hungary Inge in 1928 in Shanghai, Japanese samurai in the 1940s in Beijing; Zhao Daoxin (1908–1990, Xingyi Quan, a student of Wang Xiangzhai), beat Norwegian Andersen in 1930 in Shanghai; Li Yongzong (a student of Wang Xiangzhai), defeated Italian James in the 1930s in Beijing; Li Raochen (1876–1973, Sanhuang Paochui), defeated Japanese samurai at the end of the 1930s in Beijing and Japanese samurai in the 1940s in Nanjing; Cai Longyun (1928–present, Hua Quan), defeated Russian strongman in 1943 in Shanghai, and American boxers in 1946 in Shanghai.

Due to the lack of historical data, only the technical level and title of three foreign boxers who were defeated by Master Wang Xiangzhai are known. Hungary Inge won the world lightweight professional boxing champion and worked as a boxing coach of the Shanghai YMCA. Keniqi Takuike, a Japanese master of five Dan in Judo and four Dan in Kendo, was also defeated by Wang Xiangzhai. After that, he began to learn Yiquan. When he went back to Japan, he founded Taikiken. Norwegian Andersen, who was defeated by Zhao Daoxin, worked as the bodyguard of Song Ziwen, the minister of the finance at that time.

Through the analysis of historical records, it was found that:

The major battlefields were in China;

Foreign boxers knew little about Chinese martial arts before fighting and underestimated Chinese Wushu;

Foreign boxers were defeated by top-grade Chinese Wushu masters;

This batch of masters came from northern China, eight of whom were from Hebei province. Three men were ethnic minorities while Wang Ziping and Ma Jinbiao were Hui nationalities and Tong Zhongyi was of the Man nationality;

According to statistics on Che Yonghong, Huo Yuanjia, Han Muxia, Wang Ziping, Chen Zizheng, Sun Lutang, Tong Zhongyi,

Photo of Cai Longyun (right) and the author of this book, Beijing, April, 1998

Ji Wanshan and Wang Xiangzhai, the first time they defeated the foreign boxers, their average age was 47.2 years old, while Sun Lutang was a 69-year-old man when he beat six Japanese samurai in Shanghai;

Eight of the 15 Wushu masters practiced Shaolinquan, five men used Xingyiquan and one studied Taijiquan.

At the time, foreign boxers who came to China were very arrogant and supercilious. In the fall of 1925, a batch of Japanese judo masters gave an open challenge at Kunshan park of Hongkou District, Shanghai. They wrote such phrases such as "no competitor of fists in east Asia, kicking China shows invincible might" and "smash all enemy resistance." However, Chinese master Tong Zhongyi defeated a Japanese samurai and broke the enemy's spirit.

In 1930, Chinese wrestling master Yang Fawu also

Photo of Guo Huide, who defeated other foreign amateur boxes and became the champion of Shanghai boxers Match in 1931

97

defeated many Japanese judo masters, which disgraced the Japanese Mikado.

Chinese Wushu masters achieved a series of brilliant combat performances and stirred the international fighting circle.

However, some Chinese masters also fell prey to a plot by foreigners, such as Huo Yuanjia. In 1910, Japanese established a judo association in Shanghai. Many Japanese judo wrestlers in Shanghai held a grudge against Huo Yuanjia for his fame and success. They arranged competitions between Huo and some of the best judo athletes from Japan. However,

Photo of Huo Yuanjia

Huo Yuanjia, born in Xiaonanhe Village, Xiqing District, Tianjin on Jan. 19, 1869, was a patriotic martial artist and the founder of the Jing Wu Sports Federation. He defeated the foreign men of muscle in Tianjin and Shanghai by "Mizongquan" handed down from the older generations of the Huo family. His life story has been made into films many times.

all of them were defeated by Huo Yuanjia and his discipline Liu Zhensheng. The president of the judo association threw Huo Yuanjia out on the steps, and the Chinese Wushu master suffered a broken arm. The Japanese wrestlers pretended to respect Huo Yuanjia by preparing a peace-making dinner for Huo Yuanjia. A Japanese doctor invited Huo to the hospital. Huo was straight and did not suspect foul play. But, the day after Huo Yuanjia took the medicine given by the Japanese doctor, his tongue became stiff and his feet and hands tremble. A few days later, he died suddenly at the age of 41. The Japanese doctor fled back to Japan in a panic.

Chinese Wushu Going Global

Chinese Wushu has gone through three stages since the 1950s:

I. Closing stage: from the 1950s to 1960s. During this period, the Chinese Wushu circle had no connection with the international fight circle. A few Wushu delegations gave performances abroad accompanying the country's leaders.

In 1960, the China Youth Wushu Team along with the China sports delegation attended the second annual Czechoslovakia National Games Friendship evening party performance, opening the prelude to the foreign exchange of Wushu. In the same year, the Chinese Wushu team, along with a delegation to visit to Myanmar led by Zhou Enlai, went to Myanmar to perform, and won a warm welcome from the Myanmar people.

II. Demonstration stage: from the mid-1970s to mid-1980s. The Chinese Wushu circle gave public shows to various countries in the world, allowing foreigners to learn the charming nature of Chinese Wushu from the aspects of Kungfu or dancing.

In June 1974, Chinese Wushu team delegation was invited to visit Mexico and the United States. U.S. President Richard Nixon met with all the delegation members and watched a Wushu performance in front of the White House, drawing huge international attention.

In June 1974, the Japanese shadow-boxing delegation visited China. In September, the Chinese Youth Wushu delegation visited Japan.

Starting in 1982, at the invitation of some countries and regions, the Chinese Wushu Association constantly sent its best martial arts athletes and coaches to Mexico, Canada, the US, the United Kingdom, Singapore, Australia, Italy, Thailand, Hong Kong, Macao and other countries and regions for assistance in teaching, fostering a large number of martial arts backbones for them.

III. Combat exercise stage: from the mid-1980s. The foreign fight circle began assigning Chinese Wushu masters to attend international knockout tournaments or match plays. Chinese Kungfu masters are always challenged by foreign boxers when they visit abroad.

In March 1987, the first China-Japan Shadow-boxing Competition Exchange Conference was held in Beijing.

Starting from the 1990s, international Wushu competitions became increasingly frequent, greatly promoting the wushu exchange and dissemination around the world.

According to statistics, Chinese Wushu practitioners are always challenged by Japanese judoists or karate masters the most, followed by American boxers. The Japanese challenge Chinese Kungfu the most.

China and Japan are neighboring countries separated by a narrow strip of water, and both countries have made cultural exchanges for nearly a thousand years. Japan's judo and karate were deeply affected by Chinese Wushu and have earned a high reputation in the international fight circle. In addition, Shaolinquan and Taijiquan are also very popular in Japan. Japanese people are known for their strong character and being good at studying and learning from others' strong points to offset their weaknesses. Many Japanese come to China to learn Wushu. In addition, they have made many videos of masters performing different forms of Wushu, and have translated and published many books on Chinese Wushu. By studying the Quanshu (Chinese boxing schools) of Chinese Wushu, some Japanese

Photo of Putin visting Shaolin Temple, accompanied by Abbot Shi Yongxin

On Mar. 22, 2006, Russian President Vladimir Putin visited Shaolin Temple and exchanged experiences in martial arts with monks. It is well known that Putin is a black-belt judo expert.

boxers have greatly improved their skills. Some Tai Chi masters can even compete against some famous Chinese Tai Chi players. Therefore, Japanese people are the most threatening challengers to Chinese Wushu. For the past few years, Japanese teams have challenged Chinese Wushu many times but were defeated.

Muay Thai is famous for violent forms and Muay Thai masters possess a strong anti-beaten capacity. It is said that Bruce Lee, one of seven combat masters globally, had not participated in much professional combat with Muay Thai masters. Thailand has sent Muay Thai teams to China

Taiji Quan experts from 15 countries performing Taiji Quan in Xingtai

On Nov. 3, 2006, Dong Zengchen, grandson of Dong Yingjie, Chinese Taiji Quan expert, held a martial arts exchange with more than 60 foreign and Chinese apprentices in Xingtai of Hebei province in memory of the 108th anniversary of Dong Yingjie's birth. Dong Zengchen's apprentices were from 15 countries and regions including the United States, the United Kingdom and Canada.

twice, but both events have ended in failure for them. In August 2003, the Chinese team went to Thailand and defeated the Thailand team in Bangkok.

The Western boxer is noted for their strength. To date, there are no historical records on the early combat between the Chinese Wushu master and the world boxing champion. But according to some, Chinese Wushu and Western boxing have no apparent disadvantages in the fist position, so it is difficult to say which is better. In the past, when fighting the Western boxer, the Chinese Wushu master often tried to avoid the punch and moved with the opponent using flexible footwork. After outdoing the opponent's footwork, the Chinese Wushu master attacks and finally defeats the opponent using Wushu techniques. But, it is suggested if the two only combat fist strength, the Western boxer may win.

Combat is an international sport. Apart from Japan, Thailand, South Korea, many countries have their own combating techniques. For example, many countries including France, Greece, Russia, Brazil and India are famous for their combating techniques. Particularly, French leg attack techniques and Indian attack techniques have become world-famous.

In recent years, the Occident combat circles have innovatively combined Judo, Karate, Taekwondo, Muay Thai and Western boxing techniques, and this has enabled them to display enormous strength in actual combat.

Since Chinese Wushu is quickly going global, the exchanges between China and foreign countries in Wushu have greatly increased. More foreigners have come to China to learn Wushu. At the same time, some masters in Wushu have immigrated to foreign countries and taught Chinese Wushu to foreign students. The styles, skills and

Qi promoting methods have been completely exposed. Honor is simply a record of the past, not of today, nor the future. In order to brave the third challenge, Chinese Wushu circles have made many preparations.

Development of Modern Chinese Wushu

After the founding of the People's Republic of China, wushu became one of the important sports of the people, and has witnessed great advancement.

In October 1949, All-China Sports Federation was established with the approval of the State Council. In 1950, the All-China Sports Federation held a symposium on wushu in Beijing, advocating the development of wushu, and putting wushu development on the national sports agenda. In 1978, Deng Xiaoping also wrote the "good shadow-boxing" banner and donated it to Japanese friend. This inscription is not only praise for the Chinese wushu, but also a great inspiration to the world's wushu enthusiasts.

Established in 1952, the National Sports Commission listed wushu as a key event, and set up National Sports Research Society, responsible for mining, sorting, inheriting, and promoting wushu and other forms of national sports according to the guideline of "absorbing the essence and rejecting the dross," "all flowers blooms together," and "weeding through the old to bring forth the new." In 1955, based on actual work needs, the Wushu Division was set up under the sports department of the National Sports Commission. Later the division was upgraded to the Wushu Section, responsible for national wushu policy and guideline implementation, and the popularity, enhancement, and competition of wushu. In order to promote wushu development, the Wushu Research Institute of the National Sports Commission was established with the approval of the State Council. In September 1987, Wushu Section was incorporated into the Wushu Research Institute of the National Sports Commission. In May 1994, the Wushu Administration Center of the National Sports Commission was established with the overall function of the administration of wushu events.

In September 1958, the Chinese Wushu Association was established. It is the national organization of Chinese wushu, and one of the single event associations under the All-China Sports Federation. The Chinese Wushu Association has extensive exchanges and cooperation with other wushu associations around the world. Since the 1970s, the Chinese wushu delegation has toured five continents, and witnessed frequent foreign exchanges of wushu in recent years. Meanwhile, in order to promote wushu sports more extensively, the Chinese Wushu Association also provides free assistance to such developing countries in Africa, Asia and the Americas to implement wushu activities, which has been widely praised.

Modern Wushu Centers (schools)

Wushu centers (schools) are the important media of modern wushu development. With the country's vigorous support, wushu centers have gained unprecedented development after the reform and opening-up by using traditional folk wushu resources. Currently, on the Chinese mainland, there are more

Monks from Tagou School performing martial arts at Pagoda Forest to attract tourists

Students from Tagou School performing Taijiquan at 2008 Beijing Olympics opening ceremony on Aug. 8, 2008

than 12,000 wushu centers, and those in Henan, Shandong, Hebei, Anhui, and Fujian are the largest and the most influential. Henan, a great province in wushu, is the home to more than 600 wushu centers, concentrated mainly around Dengfeng Shaolin Temple and the Wenxian Chenjiagou area, known as the Holy place of Taiji.

At present, there are two major categories of wushu centers:

(I) Wushu schools relying on geographical and traditional wushu cultural advantages, integrating modern culture, science and technology education, and developing on the large scale and systematically in the group-oriented direction.

Shaolin Tagou Education Group is undoubtedly a representative around the country.

The group is located at the foot of Songshan Mountain, including Shaolin Tagou Wushu School, Songshan Shaolin Wushu Profession Institute, Shaolin Wushu International Teaching Center, Dengfeng Shaolin Secondary Vocational School, and Shaolin Middle School.

The group has evolved on the basis of the Shaoling Tagou Wushu School, which was established by Mr. Liu Baoshan in 1978. The wushu teaching majors include routines, free-boxing, boxing, taekwondo, and wushu performance with more than 400 classes. Culture teaching covers a complete education and teaching system ranging from nursery programs, primary school, junior high school, senior high school,

Chen Shaolong (right) from the United States and Chen Shaobao from Britain practicing hand slap at Chenjiagou of Wenxian county, Henan province

secondary school to university education and teaching, with more than 28,000 students at school.

Over the years, the group has been upholding the mission of "equal emphasis on cultural and wushu teaching as well as morality and skills, spreading authentic shaolin kungfu, and fostering new professionals." It attaches great importance to the all-round development of students. So far, its participants have won the title of champion at domestic and foreign competitions on many occasions.

In order for better development and dissemination of Shaolin Wushu, the Wushu performance team of the group has been invited to give wushu teaching and performances in more than 60 countries and regions around the world. At the opening and closing ceremonies of the 2008 Beijing Olympic Games and Paralympic Games, the group's performance team presented splendid wushu performances for the audiences from all over the world.

(II) Small-sized family-based and master/apprentice-based family wushu centers generally teach the kungfu of a single school of wushu.

This is one of the most ancient forms of wushu centers. With the social development, it also incorporates many modern culture elements. For example, family wushu centers have vigorously developed in Wenxian Chenjiagou. At present, Taijiquan has spread to more than 100 countries and regions around the world, and Taijiquan enthusiasts from all over the world come to visit wushu masters in Chenjiagou to become apprentices in a solemn ceremony in order to learn wushu. They are thus witnessing the combination of traditional wushu culture and the modern tourism industry, by "enjoying pastoral scenery, living in wushu masters' families, eating green fruits and vegetables, and learning authentic taiji." Family-style wushu centers are small-sized with food, accommodation, and learning services offered by the families of the wushu masters. This kind of family-style wushu center has a small number of participants, so they can gain access to the wushu masters in person.

With increasing international exchange and cooperation, quite a few wushu centers run schools in other many countries and regions, and Shaolin Temple is one of the top players. With great influence, Shaolin Temple has shaolin kungfu centers in more than 50 countries and regions around the world, having more than 3 million foreign disciples. In 2004, the House of Representatives of California passed a resolution to define March 21 each year as Songshan Shaolin Temple Day, so that California residents with different religious, ethnic and cultural backgrounds can enjoy Shaolin Zen Buddhism and wushu culture with a long history.

Wushu Education at Colleges and Universities

The cultural identity of wushu is the root cause of the spread of wushu since ancient times, while the inheritance and development of any kind of culture are inseparable from education. To enable Chinese wushu to really go global, it must be incorporated into the formal education system.

In 1954, the National Sports Commission set up a competition for coaching wushu teams at the Central Sports Institute (now Beijing Sport University). In August 1958, the National Sports Commission convened in Qingdao for the National Sports College President Forum. After the forum, Beijing Sport University and Shanghai University of Sport set up wushu departments in succession, marking the formal entry of wushu into higher education. In 1961, the National Sports Commission experts prepared *Wushu*, the first handout for national sports institute undergraduates. In 1963, Beijing Sport University began to offer graduate programs, marking a new stage of wushu education.

Since the reform and opening-up in 1978, more and more colleges and universities have established wushu departments, with enrollment scopes and levels expanding constantly, covering graduate, undergraduate, junior college, and correspondence programs as well as ongoing education for coaches and various kinds of short courses for Chinese and foreign wushu staff. A diversified wushu talent cultivation system has formed initially.

So far, more than 40 colleges and universities have obtained the right to confer a master's degree in wushu. In April 1996, the Academic Degrees Committee of the State Council approved Shanghai University of Sport to become the first site to confer a doctoral degree of wushu, followed by Beijing Sport University, East China Normal University, and South China Normal University, which obtained the right to confer a doctoral degree of wushu.

In July 1998, the undergraduate education program outline issued by the Ministry of Education set up a major of "national traditional sports," a newly established undergraduate program as a secondary discipline of physical education. At present, the discipline mainly covers three research orientations: wushu competitive sports, wushu culture and education, as well as folk sports and traditional regimen, and the cultivation orientation is divided mainly into wushu routines (with teaching contents focusing on competitive wushu routines) and wushu fighting (focusing on competitive wushu free boxing). For decades, colleges and universities have fostered lots of wushu professionals and teaching resources, as well as high-level wushu cultural researchers, making tremendous contributions to the development of wushu.

After the return of Hong Kong in 1997, wushu education

witnessed great development. In the autumn of 2003, IVE Chai Wan set up wushu programs, teaching mainly taijiquan, along with other wushu routines, marking the first entry into higher learning institutions in Hong Kong, and having a positive influence on the further development of wushu in Hong Kong, and even in promoting wushu development in Hong Kong, Macao and Southeast Asian countries.

Wushu Competitions and Olympic Performance Events

After the founding of the People's Republic of China, a growing number of wushu competitions played a vital role in mining and sorting out wushu heritage, and promoting wushu development.

In September 1959, the first National Games was held in Beijing with 172 athletes from 25 provinces and cities attending wushu competition events and performance events.

Women players Fu Shuyun (right) and Liu Yuhua performing sanhe sword at the 11th Olympic Games in 1936

Qin Lizi (in red) defeated Mary Jane Estimar from the Philippines and claimed the gold in the women's 52 kg category of Sanshou at the 2008 Beijing Olympic Games on Aug. 24, 2008

In September 1982, the Chinese Wushu International Friendship Invitational Tournament was held in Nanjing, involving five teams of 41 athletes from the United States, Canada, the Philippines, Hong Kong and Chinese mainland.

In August 1985, the First International Wushu Invitational Tournament was held in Xi'an, which was the first of its kind organized by China, and witnessed 89 athletes from 17 national and regional teams.

In October 1990, wushu was listed as an official competition event at the 11th Asian Games held in Beijing. Some 96 athletes from 11 countries and regions were present.

In October 1991, the First World Wushu Championships were held in Beijing. A total of 500-plus athletes from 40 countries and regions took part in wushu routines and free-boxing competitions. The championships are held biennially.

In August 1993, the First Annual National Wushu Hometown Competition was held in Wenxian county, Henan. The competition is held biennially.

In October 1996, the Third Annual National Farmers' Games was held in Shanghai, and Wushu was listed as competitive event.

In May 1999, the First International Traditional Wushu and Stunt Competition was held in Taizhou, Zhejiang.

In July 2002, the First World Cup Wushu Free-boxing Competition was held in Shanghai. The competition is held biennially.

In February 2006, the First International Wushu Fighting King Competition was held in Chongqing. The competition is held annually.

In July 2009, the Eighth Annual World Games were held in Kaohsiung, Taiwan, and wushu was listed as an official event.

For a long time, wushu enthusiasts and supporters have been working hard, hoping to witness the entry of the several-thousand-year-old sports into the Olympic family.

As early as 1936, Chinese wushu made its Olympic Games debut at Berlin. The Chinese Wushu Performance Group, consisting of Zhang Wenguang, Wen Jingming, Zheng Huaixian, Jin Shisheng, Zhang Erding, Kou Yunxing, Zhai Lianyuan, Fu Shuyun, and Liu Yuhua et al, conquered western audiences with their splendid performance in Hamburg, Frankfurt, Berlin and other cities in Germany.

Zhai Lianyuan attending Kung Fu performance at the 11th Olympic Games in 1936

After the founding of the People's Republic of China in 1949, the government sent wushu delegations abroad to visit and give wushu performances, expanding the influence of wushu in the world arena.

In October 1984, the Chinese Wushu Association invited heads of wushu organizations in 12 countries and regions including

France, the Federal Republic of Germany, Italy, Japan, and the United States to hold an international wushu symposium in Wuhan, discussing the further development of wushu around the world and other issues, and jointly signed a memorandum. Everyone agreed to establish an international wushu organization led by China as soon as possible.

In August 1985, the Preparatory Committee for the International Wushu Federation (IWF) was formally established in Xi'an. Subsequently, the representatives of the five member states—China, United Kingdom, Italy, Japan and Singapore —held the first meeting, electing Xu Cai as the director of the Preparatory Committee. The Secretariat of the Preparatory Committee was located in Beijing, China.

In October 1990, IWF was established and headquartered in Beijing.

After the establishment of the IWF, World Wushu Championships were held every two years. The First World Wushu Championships were held in Beijing in October 1991.

In October 1994, the 28th International Sports Federation was held in Monaco, and IWF was accepted as a formal member. In June 1999, the IWF was temporarily recognized by the International Olympic Committee (IOC). In December 2001, IWF signed an agreement with the World Anti-Doping Agency (WADA). In February 2002, the 113th Plenary Meeting of the IOC adopted the decision to officially recognize the IWF, and wushu to become a sports event. Now IWF has 120 member countries and regions in five continents.

After Beijing's successful bid for hosting the 2008 Olympic Games, the IWF submitted in December 2001 the formal application to IOC to include wushu in the Olympic events, and the application won great support of the ICO. The IOC agreed to take wushu as a performance event at the 2008 Olympic Games, setting a total of 15 events, 10 gold medals for routines and five gold medals for free-boxing.

The competition was held in Beijing from Aug. 21 to Aug. 24, 2008. Some 128 athletes from 43 countries and regions joined the competition, and the Chinese team ranked first with eight gold medals.

It is only a start that wushu became a performance event. To become an official Olympic event, wushu still has a long way to go.

Folk Wushu Development

Over thousands of years, wushu has been spreading silently, and growing firmly on the vast land of China. With social development, wushu gains its development with access to colleges and competition arenas. In the modern society, wushu, a traditional Chinese sport, is showing the trend of diversified development. However, the most colorful, dynamic, and vital

Photo of Wu Tunan, Taijiquan expert, and Li Ziming (right), Bagua Palm experts at Beijing on Jun. 10, 1984

Li Ziming (1902–1993) was the Baguaquan successor of the third generation and served as the first president of Beijing Baguaquan Research Association.

is the folk traditional wushu—the root of the development of Chinese wushu. The Chinese government has always attached great importance to the mining, sorting, inheritance and development of folk wushu.

In November 1953, the National Folk Sports Performance and Competition was held in Tianjin, marking the first of its kind after the founding of the People's Republic of China. A total of 145 athletes joined the performance and competition of 332 events including Chinese boxing, wushu weapons, fights, and short weapons, serving as a significant display of folk wushu.

In September 1958, the Chinese Wushu Association was established in Beijing, followed by other provinces and municipalities. Folk wushu is also included in the management of the Chinese Wushu Association.

In January 1979, the National Sports Commission issued the circular on mining and sorting out wushu heritage. In May of the same year, the First National Wushu Exchange was held in Nanning, Guangxi. Some 284 athletes from 29 provinces, autonomous regions and municipalities, as well as Hong Kong and Macao, staged performances involving more than 510 performances. Then the concept of the traditional wushu began to appear in the wushu domain. From 1983 to 1986, the work in this regard branched out around China to make a top-down survey of the folk wushu, and find traditional wushu techniques. The work was fruitful: 129 boxing varieties were discovered in various places with explicit sources and rules, and unique styles and systems; 6.51 million Chinese characters of theories and books in various provinces and municipalities; 395 hours of video recordings of veteran masters and techniques, as well as a lot of other literatures and ancient weapons.

In early 1982, the first domestic private wushu organizations —Beijing Baguazhang Research Association—was established. Upon its establishment, the association mined the Dong Haichuan tombstone and moved the tomb, causing great influence at that time. Later, it organized reports to enable Baguazhang of various schools to display their own techniques, set up tutoring stations in various parks to teach Baguazhang free of charge, carried out memorial activities to show respect for teaching, and organized domestic Baguazhang competitions.

Since then, almost all of the schools of Chinese boxing established research societies, for example, Yang Style Taijiquan Society, Chen Style Taijiquan Society, Wu Style Taijiquan Society, Sun Style Taijiquan Society, and Xingyiquan Research Society in Beijing, Yang Style Taijiquan Association and Xingyiquan Research Society in Shanxi, and Jianquan Taijiquan Society and Chin Woo Athletic Federation in Shanghai. These folk wushu organizations play a great role in the dissemination of folk wushu and promotion of a national fitness campaign.

With the development of folk wushu, international wushu festivals and wushu invitational tournaments emerged, including the Zhengzhou International Shaolin Wushu Festival, Yongnian International Taijiquan Association, Henan Wenxian International Taijiquan Annual Summit, Shanxi Traditional Yang Style Taijiquan International Invitational Tournament, Cangzhou Wushu Festival, and Shanxi Xingyiquan Invitational Tournament. At present, the World Traditional Wushu Festival is the most influential. Starting from 2004, the festival has run three sessions. All of these play a positive role in promoting the spread of folk wushu.

Development Tendency

The following period of history will be a prosperous time for Chinese Wushu and also an era of large-scale competition, with a lot of weeding out and merging—both are part of historical inevitability, and also follow the trend of the times. It is anticipated the 21st century will turn over an unusual leaf for Chinese Wushu history.

Chinese Wushu holds a unique national culture pattern, which integrates body-building, combating and aesthetics. Its future growth will be based on the national culture traditions and follow the inherent laws of Wushu to move forward. The body-building, combating and aesthetics are the basic social functions of Wushu, which pays attention to different historical periods. Between the 1950s and

Yang Fengtang (1896–1974) performing Xinyi Liuhequan

the mid-1980s, Wushu gave profound attention to its aesthetics and presented many new set exercises (mostly Changquan). Since the 1980s, Wushu has given top priority to its combat techniques, which is closely connected with the promotion of free-style combat and the frequent exchanges between China and foreign countries. However, great importance has always been attached to the body-building function by the populace. Especially after the early 1980s, the Taiji craze is a typical example.

In the future, more importance will be given to the functions of body-building and combat. Chinese Wushu will grow quicker and become more practical under the guidance of the commodity economy. The aesthetics function is also very important as it is still a form of mental enjoyment, or consumption.

Among various schools of Quan, the Neijiaquan (internal martial arts) is most vigorous. The internal martial arts closely integrate combat with body-building, and exercises with health-preserving. Apart from apparent health-preserving and body-building functions, it allows a smaller force to beat a larger one by using combat techniques. It has swept across the country quickly, between only one and two centuries. It is not the casual result of history. In view of the aesthetic value, besides the Baguazhang, the internal martial arts have no advantage. For example, Taijiquan is weak in aesthetic value, while the Xingyiquan almost has no such value. Meanwhile, the Yiquan has neither set exercises, nor aesthetic value. However, those schools of Quan without aesthetic value grow fast and spread wide.

According to the writer, Chinese Wushu will still continue to grow in simple and practical styles for a long period of time in future. Wushu will highlight its practical value at the expense of part of its aesthetic value. Of course, that does not mean Wushu will eliminate the "dance" element completely, as it depends on it to form the uniform rating criteria to practice Wushu globally, and enter major competitions such as the Olympic Games.

In the future, all schools of Quan of the Chinese Wushu will face severe tests. A large number of set exercises will be eliminated during actual combat. Some will be simplified or improved. Some schools of Quan will face the grim problem of existence. Under the combination of various schools of Quan, some new schools and set exercises will come on stage. They will be featured by simple

Cai Longyun performing Huaquan in Zhengzhou, Henan in 1983

Cai Longyun is a famous martial artist and serves as vice president of the Chinese Wushu Association and assistant professor of the Shanghai Physical Education Institute. He is good at Huaquan, Shaolinquan, Taijiquan and Xingyiquan.

(X) Feeling like the body is floating or sinking is normal when practicing the internal martial arts. If you feel dizzy during *Zhoutian gong* (a kind of internal martial arts) practice, stop and have your blood pressure examined. People who have the hypertensive cerebral symptom are not fit to exercise *Zhoutian gong*.

(XI) Great importance should be given to position training, but avoid excessive training at the beginning.

(XII) Equal attention should be given to the simple movements, including Chongquan (front punch) and *tan ti* (front kick).

(XIII) Do not seek highly difficult or impossible moves right away.

(XIV) Concentrate, focus and pay close attention to learning every detail during practice.

(XV) Do not argue with superiors.

(XVI) Do strike hit trees, walls or hard objects with any part of the body.

(XVII) Pay special attention to training involving the crotch, elbows, shoulders and knees.

(XVIII) Stay modest at all times and do not despise anyone at any time.

(XIX) Do not practice martial arts when exhausted, and do not practice internal marital arts when the mood is cannot remain calm from great sorrow, rage, or joy.

(XX) Assure enough sleep, increase nutrition and use hot water to wash your feet.

Appendix II
Chronological Table of the Chinese Dynasties

The Paleolithic Period	Approx. 1,700,000–10,000 years ago
The Neolithic Age	Approx. 10,000–4,000 years ago
Xia Dynasty	2070–1600 BC
Shang Dynasty	1600–1046 BC
Western Zhou Dynasty	1046–771 BC
Spring and Autumn Period	770–476 BC
Warring States Period	475–221 BC
Qin Dynasty	221–206 BC
Western Han Dynasty	206 BC–AD 25
Eastern Han Dynasty	25–220
Three Kingdoms	220–280
Western Jin Dynasty	265–317
Eastern Jin Dynasty	317–420
Northern and Southern Dynasties	420–589
Sui Dynasty	581–618
Tang Dynasty	618–907
Five Dynasties	907–960
Northern Song Dynasty	960–1127
Southern Song Dynasty	1127–1279
Yuan Dynasty	1206–1368
Ming Dynasty	1368–1644
Qing Dynasty	1616–1911
Republic of China	1912–1949
People's Republic of China	Founded in 1949